Contents

Acknowledgements

This paper is the result of the efforts of numerous people, and clearly we cannot name everyone concerned. However, our particular thanks go to:

Those who provided general help and advice:

Val Williams
Sue Greenwell
Alison Cleland

Those who provided comments on the early draft:

Adah Kay
Christine Ajayi
Rachel Hodgkin
Juliette Patrick
Janice Funnell
Elizabeth Jones
Denny Grant
Mel Lloyd-Smith
Barry Troyna
Anne Sinclair-Taylor
Eric Sainsbury
Helen Roberts

The FSU Education/Social Policy Group played a crucial part throughout:

Sue Milne
Susannah Wood

Gwyneth Williams
Pam Bromley
Lynne Mackey
Peter Postlewaite
Jaqui Ragoonath
Yvonne Bailey-Smith

Anne Gold provided invaluable advice and consultation throughout.

Many Barnardo's staff contributed and assisted, particularly:

Rosie Tomlinson and colleagues
Sarah Wellard
Carol Belk
Betty Golightly (Research Secretary)

A special thank you to our co-authors Laura Ashworth and Maud Blair, who also provided help, advice and comments at various stages.

Most of all, our thanks go to the thirty children and their families who provided the case material for the study. We would like to believe that the study will benefit others in such circumstances in the future.

Ruth Cohen, Family Service Units
Mike Hughes, Barnardo's

Foreword

Education is a basic human right. Exclusion from school is a denial of that right. As organisations working to promote children's rights and the well-being of families, Barnardo's and Family Service Units are concerned about the rise in numbers of children excluded from school. This study, published in the early months of International Year of the Family, raises important questions about current education policies and how they affect families.

Barnardo's and FSU have collaborated in this study. We share the view that families should be enabled to speak out on their own behalf and be heard; we provide services which aim to support parents and children, and to help them increase control over their own lives.

Education is at the forefront of public debate. Within this debate there is one voice which is often missing: that of the parents and pupils themselves, especially those coping with disadvantage. This report considers exclusion from their point of view.

We believe that reversing the escalation of exclusions must be a priority for policy makers and practitioners, and welcome the recent changes in law and guidance as a recognition of the problem. We do not see any one group or institution as solely responsible for this phenomenon. Our interest, indeed, is not in allocating blame but in looking for constructive responses and solutions: and we hope that Government, schools, other agencies and families can all cooperate in this.

Adah Kay
Family Service Units

Roger Singleton
Barnardo's

Introduction

Why this report?

Barnardo's and Family Service Units both provide social welfare services to children and families experiencing difficulties of various kinds: difficulties which often relate to poverty, disadvantage and discrimination.

This joint report arose initially from profound concerns expressed in both agencies by workers on the ground. These concerns were stimulated not by national policy debates, but by workers' own experience of working with children and families. They found themselves increasingly dealing with problems relating to exclusion from school, which seemed often to affect Black[1] families more frequently than White.

A major focus of the report is how exclusion is perceived by, and affects, parents and pupils in touch with Barnardo's and FSU. It does not aim to examine the other "side of the coin": exclusion from the perspective of the school or education authority. This would not be appropriate or practicable as we are not mainstream education providers. However, we wholeheartedly acknowledge the extreme pressures on schools and teachers which form a backcloth to the increase in exclusions.

We feel that the voice and experience of parents and pupils affected by exclusion is missing from the debate, and this is what we have

---

[1] In this report we use the term "Black" to refer to people who identify themselves as African, Asian, African-Caribbean or mixed race origin, unless otherwise specified. We recognise the limitations of this definition, but for the purposes of this study it was the most practical option.

sought to provide. We would not suggest that we are providing the whole picture on exclusion, and indeed accept that in many of the cases we cite, the teacher or school might want to tell a very different story. But we believe that the perspective we present provides a crucial additional dimension which must be taken into account.

It is also important to register at the outset that the case studies reported do not reflect the full range of excluded pupils and their families but rather some of the more vulnerable and disadvantaged within that range. As we explain in chapter four, the high proportion in our cases of pupils with special educational needs, and of families on low incomes, relates at least in part to the characteristics of families using our services and the reasons why they sought our help. But though they do not provide a cross-section of excluded pupils, the cases studied do highlight some important issues. In particular, they include some Black families, which we think is essential given the disproportionate exclusion of African-Caribbean boys registered in the official statistics. The study reinforces the need to investigate further the causes of this phenomenon.

What is in the report

In Part One we set out the wider context of exclusion: chapter one provides an overview of previous research evidence on exclusion. We then (in chapter two) examine policy and other developments relevant to the increase in exclusions. In chapter three Laura Ashworth of the Advisory Centre for Education (ACE) reviews the available statistical evidence on exclusion, and the conclusions that can be drawn from it. She also reports on research carried out by ACE, including an analysis of concerns about exclusion expressed by parents seeking their help.

Part Two focuses on qualitative case material from Barnardo's and FSU. In chapter four 30 case studies submitted by workers from the two agencies are summarised. This is followed in chapters five and six by an analysis of the crucial issues emerging from interviews with six Black and six White pupils and their parents drawn from the 30 cases. Maud Blair of the Open University carried out the interviews with Black families and contributed chapter five. The principal findings are summarised in chapter seven.

In Part Three, the focus moves to a discussion of these findings (chapter eight). This is followed by more general policy comments in chapter nine. Clear recommendations arise from our study, and these are further summarised in chapter ten. They point to areas of concern in both policy and practice, they are realistic in their dimensions, and they represent the minimum which we believe is needed in order to reverse the trend of the extensive use of exclusion.

Finally, in an Afterword, Sir Peter Newsam of London University's Institute of Education comments on the paper and reminds the reader that some problems are timeless, although recently they have increased enormously in significance.

PART ONE
BACKGROUND

1. Literature Review

Which children get excluded?

Exclusion from school affects two groups of children, both of which receive attention in this study: first, those who have learning disabilities, including those whose ability to learn is impaired by emotional or behavioural difficulties; secondly, those whose behaviour is considered disruptive, and where the school system is unable to maintain them. The exclusion of either can give cause for concern, and in many instances both descriptions apply to a child. However, the causative and associative factors may be different, and to a point the two issues must be treated separately.

Facts about exclusion

A most useful summary of the principal issues associated with exclusion is offered by Pippa John (1993). Her references cover a period of some 25 years, and it is therefore possible that some of the phenomena to which she refers have now assumed different aspects or proportions. She says that:

- exclusion is three times more frequent in secondary schools than primary.
  This may have changed in recent years – The Department for Education (DFE 1992) suggests that primary school exclusions represent 13% of the total.
- many excluded pupils have difficult home circumstances.
- whether or not a statement of needs is in operation, many pupils who are excluded because of behaviour are also experiencing difficulties in learning.

- exclusion can engender either feelings of rejection in the pupil, or unhealthy feelings of being in control of events.
- exclusion does not generally occur because of one incident; rather it is triggered by a last straw event which is at the end of a culminating string.
- the ethos and culture of the school has a significant effect on the extent of exclusion.

Why have exclusions increased in number?

No one doubts that exclusions have increased. Evidence from the Department for Education (DFE 1993a) and OFSTED (OFSTED 1993a) shows a rise between 1990 and 1992. This is part of a longer term trend; for example, Lloyd-Smith (Lloyd-Smith 1993) refers to a study in which it was found that there had been an increase of 285% in the phenomenon in Birmingham in 16 years, while the general population of the area had dropped by 28%.

Stirling (1992) argues that the increase in exclusion is largely due to the effects of the Education Reform Act on school management:

"Mainstream Heads .... were all concerned that the publication of test results should give a favourable impression of their school. 'Kids who screw up the formula are not going to be encouraged.' "

Lloyd-Smith (1993) too draws attention to the utility of exclusion to heads and governors as a means of selection and regulation.

Stirling also (1993) points out that schools are faced with a difficult choice: the difficult pupil must either be seen as an object of punishment or a drain on resources:

"Either the school can consider that the child having broken school rules should be disciplined, the ultimate punishment being expulsion; or that the child has a requirement for extra educational resources."

Three further main strands of causation are considered in the literature: first, Furlong (1985) suggests that domestic and community deprivation is associated with increase in disruptive behaviour in school. Lloyd-Smith also refers to the popular belief that an alleged breakdown of societal discipline has spilled over into school.

Secondly, Garner (1993), referring to the work of Rutter et al. (1979) and Graham (1988) argues that

".... far from being a neutral backcloth against which students engage in a varied series of social and academic interactions, the organisation and ethos of the school itself is a crucial determinant of student behaviour."

Thirdly, Peagam (1991) in his study of 27 Local Education Authorities considered the association between a high level of statementing for emotional and behavioural difficulties and a low exclusion rate. He found that there was no clear link, thereby casting doubt on statementing as a means of affecting attitudes and practice positively.

African-Caribbean Pupils

The over-representation of African-Caribbean male pupils among those excluded should be seen in the context of general inequalities in school achievement, and especially of the under-achievement of African-Caribbean pupils (see for example Education for All, HMSO 1985). Also in 1985 the Commission for Racial Equality found in their Birmingham study that 43% of those excluded from school were West Indian (sic), where West Indians were 9% of the population.

There has been much discussion of causation and of possible solutions, but recent research focusing on how Black pupils are dealt with in the school, and highlighting their experience of differential treatment, is particularly relevant when considering reasons for ethnic differences in exclusion.

Gillborn (1990) notes that

".... as a group, pupils of Afro-Caribbean ethnic origin experience more conflictual teacher-pupil relationships than their peers of other ethnic origins....concern that the levels of suspensions and expulsions of Afro-Caribbean pupils is becoming a familiar feature of the educational world."

He describes the processes whereby certain behaviours amongst this ethnic group generate much more rapid disciplinary action than amongst white counter-parts. He illustrates this by describing a series of incidents at the school at which he conducted his study, leading to serious sanctions being invoked against a group of three African-Caribbean boys:

"Teachers' perspectives concerning the myth of an Afro-Caribbean challenge operated in such a way that any offence by an Afro-Caribbean pupil could be interpreted as indicative of a more general "attitude" (an "inner drive"). In the case of this Afro-Caribbean male clique, which rejoiced in both the ethnicity and the physical independence of its members, the processes were amplified until the school took very serious official action against the three in the form of suspensions and even an expulsion."

Similarly, Wood and Hammersley (1993) offer evidence that Black pupils are more likely to be excluded than White pupils for perpetrating similar infringements.

While explanations for the phenomenon vary, there is wide consensus that this serious issue of race requires urgent attention. Whether this applies to all Black pupils or only to those of African-Caribbean origin needs further examination:

"There is clearly some support for the argument that the construction and belief in an Afro-Caribbean male stereotype may contribute to the high rates of exclusions from school experienced by such pupils. The extent to which this process holds true for Asian pupils must remain speculative at this stage." (Blyth and Milner 1993)

What are the consequences of exclusion to the child?

Blyth and Milner are concerned that the net effect for the child is that he or she disappears from the system:

"....a sizeable proportion of permanently excluded pupils simply disappear from the educational system. Relatively few permanently excluded pupils appear to be provided with a place at another mainstream school. Head teachers appear to be increasingly reluctant to accept pupils excluded from other schools."

Secondly, there is an increased likelihood of excluded children being drawn into the statutory child protection system (Bennathan 1992).

Most importantly, the phenomenon of exclusion highlights the fact that in our educational system the child is not generally recognised as the consumer of the service. This is both cause and effect. As well as highlighting a civil rights issue, exclusion is also aggravated by the fact, according to Blyth and Milner, that for the pupil there is an "absence of a legitimate avenue for the expression of consumer opinion and choice." In this context, difficult behaviour may "appropriately be understood as a measure of customer satisfaction with current educational provision."

Taking the civil rights issue a point further, the exclusion from school may be interpreted as an aspect of civic or social exclusion.

Professional responses to the problem

Longley and Newsome (1988) say that much can be achieved by clarity and good communication. Systems need to be brought into play to ensure that an act of discipline is distinct (for example distinguishing between fixed term or permanent exclusion) and properly communicated.

".... there were two major problems. The first was the uncertainty in schools as to the differences between suspensions and exclusions. The second was the inaccurate reporting, largely caused by the use of one inadequate form for reporting both types of debarment."

They describe their establishment of procedures and information systems within a local authority, aimed at improving relationships within the school, between the school staff and the governing body, and between school and psychological service.

This and other professional responses are heartening. John's (1993) study showed that the problem is not intractable, and that school management may have an impact on the extent of exclusion. The more controlling the school, the greater the likelihood of extensive exclusion. Wright referred to

"the level within a school hierarchy at which the decision-making power is exercised. In low-suspending schools form tutors tended to have more responsibility. It was expected that problems would be sorted out at the lowest possible level."

The need for further study and development work is clearly needed, to ensure that the most positive and supportive ethos and culture are developed within the school setting. Perhaps too there is scope to consider the value of a counselling service in this context.

2. The Policy Context

Introduction

The 1980s and early 1990s saw a large-scale upheaval in school organisation, funding, curriculum, and in the system of examinations and pupil assessments. Alongside this there were major battles over ideas about educational methods and the functions and responsibilities of teachers, in which the teaching profession and education planners often found themselves at odds with Government policymakers. This all took place against a background of restraints on local authority funding affecting spending on education alongside other services, and of other important social changes This section provides a brief overview of these developments, and also explains changes in the law covering exclusion from school.

The social context

Before turning to education policy, it is useful briefly to refer to wider social changes affecting school pupils and their families over the 80s and 90s. A major relevant development has been the massive rise in child poverty. The latest figures show that in 1991 31% of children were living in families with below 50% of average income – a three-fold increase since 1979. In 1989, a quarter of all children (2.8 million) were living at or below the income support level (Kumar 1993). The links between poverty and other forms of deprivation such as ill-health and educational underachievement are now well documented (see for example summary in Kumar).

Of recent years there have also been major structural changes in employment patterns. Mass unemployment is now a permanent

link with underachievement vicious circle

feature, particularly among school-leavers and young people, and disproportionately affecting Black people (Unemployment Unit and Youthaid 1993). And since 1988 most unemployed 16 and 17 year olds have not been eligible for state benefits.

As widely publicised in recent months, family and employment patterns have changed over the last 30 years, with many more children being brought up for at least part of their school life in lone parent households, and many more mothers going out to work. However unlike the other changes described above, this is a longer-term shift whose effects would have begun to be felt well before the recent period.

Education reforms: market forces

Education reforms of the 1980s and early 90s were designed to introduce a "market" philosophy into education, whereby schools' competition for pupils was intended to improve educational performance. This was to be achieved through several linked reforms.

School funding is now tied closely to pupil numbers, greatly reducing LEA discretion to take account of variations in social need. Combined with a move to open enrolment, whereby schools have to accept pupils if there are spare places, this means that – given falling rolls – they must compete for pupils in order to retain funds. Competition has been further emphasised by publication of "league tables" covering results of Standard Assessment Tests (SATs), examination results and truancy. Alongside this has gone increasing devolution of management, and especially of funding, to schools, and the encouragement of "opting out" of LEA control. The 1993 Education Act made it clear that it is planned for LEAs to retain at most a residual role: even their basic responsibility for providing school places will be taken over by a "funding association" if enough schools in their area opt out.

In this market-oriented environment, schools needing to present an attractive image to parents have to compete over pupil standards and academic achievement. It has been suggested that difficult or low-achieving pupils may well be the "unsaleable goods" in the market-place (Lloyd-Bennett 1993). The education reforms also provide a striking contrast to the Children Act 1989, which reshaped the law affecting children's welfare. The Act's overriding principle is that the child's welfare must be *paramount* in any court proceedings; and it introduces a duty to ascertain the wishes and feelings of the child when making decisions affecting them. This is consistent with the U.N. Convention on the Rights of the Child, which the the British Government has ratified. Article 12 provides that children capable of forming a view have the right to express it, and that view should be given due weight in accordance with their age and maturity. Article three promulgates the principle that the child's interests must have primary consideration.

Yet education legislation is framed in terms of parents' rather than children's rights; giving the child her/himself no right to education, nor to be heard in proceedings such as appeals against exclusion.

Special educational needs

The 1980s also saw major changes in this area. The 1981 Education Act aimed to revolutionise provision for pupils with special educational needs. It argued for their inclusion in mainstream schooling wherever possible, and encouraged the concept of a continuum of need, within which it was then estimated that 20% of pupils might have special needs at some stage in their school career, but only 2% would require assessment resulting in a "statement of special educational needs", which gave them a legal right to specified additional support. The ethos of the 1981 Act is arguably at odds with the education reforms discussed above. It has been pointed out that "... there may be longer-term costs involved [for mainstream schools] in giving too high a profile to SEN; market image, national testing performance and staying on rates in the 6th form may conspire to produce new kinds of exclusion or marginalisation for SEN students (Bowe and Ball with Gold 1992).

There has in any case been considerable criticism of LEAs' implementation of the 1981 Act (eg Audit Commission 1992) and a major issue has been the lack of resources to implement it: leading to a pressure to produce statements which are "resource-led" rather than "needs-led". Baroness Warnock, whose influential report led to the 1981 Act, has herself acknowledged that it is not working, expressing concern that pupils with emotional and behavioural difficulties may not be receiving help, and may therefore be excluded (TES 1992). Overall funding restrictions and the devolution of funds to individual schools may already have affected the level of SEN provision: for example both Barnardo's and FSU have reported local cutbacks in SEN support (Barnardo's 1992, FSU 1992), and this could become more prevalent as the movement of finance and control from LEAs to schools is strengthened by the provisions of the 1993 Education Act. Specific concern has been expressed about a possible decline in the importance of specialist teachers working with SENs in mainstream schools (see eg Gains 1993). And with leaked DFE predictions that statements are likely to increase by 60% between 1992 and 1997, it is hard to see how resources for special needs can keep pace (*Special Children* 1993).

The 1993 Education Act contains a section on special educational needs, in particular introducing a code of practice for schools and local authorities to be issued by the Secretary of State, prescribing time limits to speed up the statementing process and widening appeal rights, including setting up a new special educational needs tribunals. The draft code of practice issued for consultation includes a welcome emphasis on the importance of taking into account the ascertainable wishes of the pupil (DFE 1993b).

Exclusion policy

In England and Wales, the accepted terminology prior to 1986 was that pupils ordered to leave school temporarily were "suspended", and those ordered out permanently were "expelled". The 1986 (no. 2) Education Act replaced this with the term "exclusion" covering both situations. It provided for three types of exclusion: *fixed-term* where a date for return is given, *indefinite* where no date is given but the case is to be investigated and *permanent* where the pupil cannot return to the school in question. The Act also provided clear appeals procedures and required schools to inform parents (in all exclusion cases), as well as governors and the LEA (in all cases except very brief fixed term exclusions). It was hoped that this would clarify the rules and the rights of pupils and parents, and help to avoid the drastic measure of permanent exclusion (Lloyd-Smith 1993).

Following concern about the widely-acknowledged increase in all types of exclusion discussed in the next chapter the DFE issued a discussion paper on exclusions late in 1992, following this speedily with amendments to the 1993 Education Act. The Act provides that

Changed now enough

indefinite exclusions will be abolished from September 1994, and fixed term exclusions will only be allowed for up to 15 days in a term. Where an excluded pupil is receiving education elsewhere – at another school, in a special unit or otherwise – the funding for them will immediately be transferred there from the excluding school. LEAs will also have a duty to secure pupils' education while they are excluded. Additionally, there will be increased regulations covering special off-site units for excluded pupils – to be known as pupil referral units – although they will not have to operate the full national curriculum. The DFE will also issue further regulations on exclusion, backed by guidance to schools aimed to encourage them to use exclusion as a last resort.

Scottish law on exclusion is more specific than that for England and Wales. A pupil may be excluded either where he or she does not comply with the school rules; or where allowing them to continue at the school would be likely to be seriously detrimental to order and discipline, or to pupils' education. There are also somewhat greater rights to information and appeal.

Other changes and pressures

Alongside the changes in school organisation and funding referred to above, teachers' work in the classroom has also been affected by other substantial changes. Since the early 1980s these have included, for example, the introduction of the GCSE examination involving course work assessment, the implementation of the national curriculum, and battles over the introduction of Standard Assessment Tests (SATs). This has been in the context of highly publicised conflicts with successive Ministers who have overtly and with relish attacked current educational methods and values and questioned the credibility of teachers' professional expertise as opposed to "common-sense" ideas about education.

Meanwhile there have been continuing restrictions on local authority spending over this period. While there are disputes about the interpretation of statistics, there has been considerable concern about the effects on schools of these financial restrictions. For example it has been calculated by the OECD that real education spending per capita declined by 1.8% per annum between 1980 and 1987 (Hutton 1992). Class size in primary schools has risen consistently since 1988

(Hansard 1993) and the condition of school buildings has been criticised (e.g. HMI 1991).

It should also be noted that teaching is now recognised as one of the most stressful of professions. Recent research found over half teachers reporting sleep difficulties, and up to a third daytime pathological symptoms (TES, 1993).

3. Making Sense of the Statistics
– Laura Ashworth, Advisory Centre for Education

Concern has been growing over the number of children excluded from school. Research has attempted to assess and quantify the trends. It has had limited success because the reporting and collection of exclusion figures has never been comprehensively achieved. There are disparities between total number of exclusions estimated by each report. ACE (1993) collected figures for 1991 from 78 local education authorities that amounted to a total of 16,595 exclusions. The NUT (1992) collected figures from 26 education authorities in May 1992 which recorded 5,300 excluded pupils. They estimated that the total number of exclusions would be 25,000 if this level was reflected in all other local authorities. A MORI survey in February/March 1992 of 79 local authorities reported 35,549 exclusions, and predicted that if all local authorities had replied the total would have been 66,315. The Department for Education (1993a) relied upon a separate reporting system that collected 2,910 reports of permanent exclusions for the year ending Summer 1991 and 3,833 for the year ending in Summer 1992; this varies with an ACE (1993) total of 5,996 permanent exclusions in 1991.

Three surveys reported trends from their figures. There was an increase of nearly a thousand exclusions recorded by the DFE (1993a) between Summer 1991 and Summer 1992. ACE (1993) reported figures over a five year period beginning with 1986. They found that the use of all types of exclusion had increased at an accelerating rate. Finally MORI (1993) reported that 80% of the local education authorities which responded to their questionnaire claimed that the number of exclusions had increased over the past two years.

Besides those children involved in formal exclusion procedures a number are excluded informally. An analysis of exclusions in Nottingham (1989) explains that sometimes parents keep their child away from school until a situation blows over, or schools will not allow a child to return to school until staff have met with the parents. ACE (1992) discovered that a third of parents who phoned their advice line with queries about exclusion procedures were asked to take their child away from school: schools failed to follow the proper procedures.

Variations in the collection and collation of figures are the most likely explanation of the statistical differences. Most reports agree that existing figures do not fully reflect the number of children who are excluded or forbidden from returning to school. The consensus seems to be that exclusions affect thousands of pupils every year and this number is growing. Perhaps if exclusion reporting were taken more seriously, this would send a signal to schools about the seriousness with which exclusions are viewed.

Research concerning the reasons which are behind the increasing use of exclusion by schools is inconclusive. There is a strong feeling that being in the market place for students encourages intolerance: MORI (1993) found that 55% of education officers blamed increased competition and the NUT (1992) found that 27% of their divisions imputed the pending league tables. However, ACE (1993) discovered that there was no correlation between the rate at which schools had been given their own budgets and the rate at which exclusions had increased. Perhaps the concept of competition is more of a feeling within schools than the actual fact of becoming an autonomous cost-centre. Another suggestion blamed lack of resources for children with special educational needs (SHA 1991/2); however, MORI (1993) found that only 3% of education authorities anticipated decreasing their spending on special needs. Other notable suggestions were lack of parental control (NUT and SHA) and poorer discipline in schools (MORI).

Variations between schools

Most of the reports agree that use of exclusion varies between schools. Different schools exclude children for different reasons and to widely differing degrees. Whereas organisations which represent the teaching professions (NUT 1992, SHA 1991/2) tend to attribute variations between schools to the social circumstances of each school's pupils, the

Department for Education asserts that the differences are too great to be explained by catchment areas and the Nottingham research noticed variations between schools which shared catchment areas. According to these two reports, effective school and classroom management cause lower use of exclusion.

School policies

Both the Secondary Heads Association (1991/2) and the Nottingham inspectorate (1989) found that behaviour in schools is good on the whole; in fact the Nottingham team found disruption in only eight out of the 89 lessons they observed. The Secondary Heads Association maintains that schools make great efforts to avoid exclusion; the Nottingham report indicates how likely their efforts are to be successful. It suggests that there is little connection between the likelihood that a discipline issue would end in exclusion and whether or not the school had a discipline policy. Most difficulties over poor behaviour were rooted in day-to-day classroom interaction, not in poor policies. Some of the work set was inappropriate for the ability of pupils. This was particularly prevalent in lessons provided by supply teachers who have lesser knowledge of the group they are expected to teach; over half of their lessons were thwarted by disruption. Schools which do not monitor classroom practice leave their teachers isolated and more likely to experience difficulties. When teachers have difficulties their pupils will too.

Some schools have a code of behaviour which clearly identifies what is acceptable and what is not. It is only fair to pupils and their parents that the school should make these things clear, and the law requires head teachers to promote good behaviour. Everyone should know how unwanted behaviour will be sanctioned and desirable behaviour praised. Unfortunately the Nottingham report (1989) noted that there was a tendency in some schools to concentrate praise on a small number of high achievers. Yet in the schools which excluded less children use of praise was more widespread.

Sanctions are better used constructively rather than just to punish. One of the most humiliating experiences for young people interviewed as part of the Nottingham survey was to be shouted at by a teacher in front of their peers. In an ACE survey of home/school issues (1993) in six out of 25 complaints about teacher attitude, parents sought advice because their child had been mocked, threatened or humiliated in front of other children. Teachers who have good interpersonal skills, particularly the ability to de-escalate confrontational situations, are less likely to belittle pupils in this way.

Some schools went as far as sending young people to spend time out (time away from the class) in a public place (Nottingham 1989). Far from allowing the pupil time to cool off, this practice cultivated resentment. Teachers in schools which excluded less pupils generally tried to de-escalate confrontations and regarded all sanctions as a learning process, thereby underlining the need to consider dignity and respect for the child when addressing issues of praise and sanctions.

Consistency

The reports cited a range of reasons for excluding a particular pupil. Most mentioned physical aggression against staff and pupils. This typically amounted to about quarter of all exclusions. However, general disobedience was the major reason for exclusion: it was described as constantly refusing to comply with school rules, verbal abuse, insolence to teachers (DFE 1992), disruption and defiance (Nottingham 1989). A child is more likely to be excluded because of a series of minor incidents rather than a single major one: 85% of Nottinghamshire exclusions for defiance and 60% of their exclusions for verbal abuse were the result of a series of incidents.

Parents who call ACE express concern about the fair application of school rules when their child has been punished for a series of minor incidents. They complain that the same punishment is meted out to all those involved in a particular incident irrespective of each child's behavioural history or the fact that pupils involved in the same incident are treated differently, or that their child's history of disobedience is dragged into all new situations. These views may contradict each other, but they do indicate that school rules may be vague and be applied inconsistently. According to pupils surveyed as part of the Nottinghamshire research inconsistency amongst staff was one of the biggest problems in school discipline. Schools may have acceptable policies but these may not be implemented in every classroom.

If a child is to be fairly excluded for a series of incidents those incidents need to be properly recorded. In the absence of record keeping, the decision to exclude is intuitive rather than reasoned. Unfortunately, poor record keeping is common (Nottingham 1989). The Local Government Ombudsman criticised a local appeal committee for accepting an exclusion report which read "Numerous incidents over a long period of time. Exceptionally bad behaviour recently, [Tom] is out of control."

Pastoral care

The upkeep and use of behavioural records are only one part of a whole child perspective. This should be fundamental to the role of the tutor. In fact schools which fail to use the child's tutor find it more difficult to achieve a consistent approach to behaviour (Nottingham 1989). Unfortunately this is common practice in schools; although most schools list "referral to tutor" within their list of sanctions, few actually invoke it. However, there is good practice to build on in many schools. Records of Achievement provide a useful framework in which pupil and tutor can jointly monitor the whole school experience, including those aspects which they find troubling (Nottingham 1989). Whilst good record keeping and monitoring will lessen unfair practice, good pastoral care will encourage respect for each individual child.

A frequently neglected aspect of pastoral care is the involvement of parents. Parents generally want to support their child's school (Nottingham 1989, ACE 1992). Many of the parents who called ACE said that the formal exclusion notice was the first time they were made aware of the difficulties their child was experiencing. ACE samples of parental opinion taken in 1990 and 1991 revealed that 50% and 70% of parents said that they had been insufficiently involved by the school before their child was excluded. From a different perspective, the Secondary Heads Association report that schools often use exclusion to create a sense of crisis in parents. The tactic seems to work, although the Nottingham research (1989) questions whether it is productive. Although early involvement was welcomed and supported by parents, parents were generally less supportive when their initial involvement came at a later stage, especially when they were informed of the trouble by the child rather than by the school.

Parental involvement after exclusion is another important matter. Parents have a right to make representations to the governing body about the head teacher's decision to exclude their child[2]. It is the opinion of the Secondary Heads Association (1991/2) that parents have become more willing in recent years to challenge exclusion decisions. Even if this is so, the statistics indicate that their efforts are ineffectual. The Secondary Heads Association reports that 88% of exclusions are upheld by the governors and DFE (1992) discovered that out of 3,000 permanent exclusions, only 200 were overturned.

The first difficulty which confronts parents is knowing that they can make representations to the governing body on any discipline matter. According to the Secondary Heads Association, governors tend to consider the decision taken by the head in all permanent exclusions but in only 44% of fixed exclusions over five days, and 78% of indefinite exclusions. Where governors fail to consider an indefinite exclusion, the child concerned may be left without schooling for a prolonged period, since an education authority only takes up responsibility for alternative education following a permanent exclusion. When a child is re-instated or returns after an indefinite or fixed exclusion, there may still be long term consequences. Exclusion practice tends to be cumulative; whatever the next behavioural difficulties, it will be viewed more seriously in the light of a previous exclusion: a fixed exclusion seldom follows an indefinite one, and fixed exclusions accumulate to justify a more serious sanction.

Next, parents will have to use the information they have received from the school as a basis for their representations. About a sixth of the parents who called ACE about their child's exclusion did not receive a letter informing them about it (ACE 1992). When schools have written, their reports to parents may also be overly negative, listing misdemeanours and omitting the preventive steps they have taken (Nottingham 1989). Parents who found out about their child's exclusion over the phone or at a meeting found this form of contact protracted, confusing, and frequently acrimonious. Where prior information has been scant or confusing, schools will obviously say more at the governors' hearing. Unless parents have accessed their child's school record, and unless this record has been diligently kept,

---

[2] The final exclusion is a decision taken by the school governors at a meeting at which the Head, the pupil and her/his parents present their cases. The governors decide whether to support or reject the Head Teachers decision to exclude. In the event of a decision to exclude, the parents are advised of their right of appeal against the decision and to submit their appeal to the local Education Office within 15 days of the Hearing.

they will be at a disadvantage. A seventh of the parents ACE (1993) advised to see their child's school record had to press their case.

Irrespective of the nature and amount of information parents received beforehand, many report to ACE (1993) that governors' exclusion hearings tend to roam across the child's whole school record rather than sticking to the one or two points which lead to the exclusion. Hearings become unbalanced; the Nottingham research (1989) says that they become insufficiently positive. The school tries to paint the child as deviant and different, rather than present an accurate and balanced picture of the whole child. Obviously it is very distressing for parents and the child to hear this sort of description. Parents who call ACE advice line (1993) also complain that governors tend to believe the accounts given by school staff rather than the child. School governors who are able to rely on good record keeping and thorough investigation are in a much better position to conduct fair hearings.

Very few parents take their case beyond the governing body, this happened in 92 out of 3,000 exclusions, and only 14 families were successful (DFE 1992). Given the catalogue of poor practice noted by ACE (1993) and the Nottingham research (1989) it would seem that parents need both accurate information and local support to argue successfully for the reinstatement of their children.

Strengthening parent involvement both before and after exclusion is an important step in protecting the welfare of children. Most reports agree that it is difficult to find an alternative placement for an excluded child, despite the laws on open enrolment (ACE 1992, Nottingham 1989). Only 29% of the 3,000 permanent exclusion recorded by the Department for Education in 1991 secured a place in another school. Other children found themselves entirely without schooling (ACE 1992), attending a special unit (22%, DFE 1992) or in home tuition (44%, DFE 1992). There is concern about the quality of part-time provision and weaknesses have been observed in curriculum content. For many young people exclusion from school will mean drastically reduced opportunities to take external exams. Although the Secondary Heads Association (1991/2) reports on the willingness of schools to accept excluded pupils, this willingness seems to be patchy: voluntary-aided and grant-maintained schools were less likely to admit excluded pupils, giving rise to fears that a species of local authority sink schools may be created. This type of development would further disadvantage children vulnerable to current trends in school discipline practice.

Some schools try to safeguard against unfair practice. These schools are mindful of both the practical steps and moral issues that protect fair play. Their behaviour codes are clear, widely known and supported by good record keeping and thorough investigation. Sanctions are seen as positive measures and there is widespread use of praise. Lessons are aimed at pupils of all abilities and pastoral care involves monitoring all aspects of each child's educational career. The school recognises that it shares its responsibility with parents who are involved at an early stage when a child is experiencing difficulties. What underlies this type of school is an ethos that respects and values each and every child.

Children who are vulnerable to unmoderated discipline procedures

Research shows that schools tend to treat different types of pupil differently. DFE (1992), Secondary Heads Association (1992) and Nottingham Education Department (1989) found that girls were three to five times less likely to be excluded than boys. African-Caribbean children were found to be disproportionately represented in exclusion statistics: the Department for Education found that they make up eight per cent of those excluded from school; this means they were four to five times more likely to be excluded than other school pupils; Nottingham Education Department deduced that African-Caribbean children were four times more likely to be excluded than white children, and ACE found that half of their advice line calls about exclusions concerned African-Caribbean children. DFE stated that 12.5% of excluded children had statements of special educational needs: ACE found that a child's special needs were a contributory factor in half the exclusions recorded on the advice line. Only the Nottingham research pursued a connection between poverty and exclusion. They found that 60% of children who are excluded live in "areas of serious or extreme disadvantage." None of the research claims that African-Caribbean children, boys, children with special educational needs or children who live in poverty behave more badly than any other part of the school population.

Not only do African-Caribbean children and children who live in poor areas figure more in the exclusion statistics, the sanctions used on them tend to be more severe. The Nottingham researchers found that nine per cent of permanent exclusions are made against children who live in advantaged areas, compared with 15% which are made against children who live in poor areas. For fixed exclusions the proportions are reversed: 56% are made against children who live in advantaged areas, whilst children who live in disadvantaged areas are only 39% of fixed exclusions. Similarly 51% of white children excluded for verbal abuse are given fixed exclusions, compared to only 43% of black children: 13% of white children are permanently excluded compared to 19% of black children (Nottingham 1989).

PART TWO
CASE EVIDENCE FROM BARNARDO'S AND FSU

This part of the report analyses case evidence from Barnardo's and FSU. Chapter 4 summarises 30 cases of excluded pupils, as reported by workers from the two agencies. All the families were in touch with local Family Service Units or Barnardo's projects.

Some of the themes arising from the cases are then explored in greater depth through analyses of interviews with a small number of White and Black parents drawn from among the case studies. Maud Blair from the Open University interviewed six Black families and reports on these in Chapter 5, while Chapter 6 concerns interviews with 6 White families carried out by Ruth Cohen from FSU. By using a Black researcher for the Black families, we hoped to explore their experiences in greater depth.

Please note that in this part all names of pupils and parents have been changed.

4. The Case Studies – Thirty Families

Introduction

Thirty case studies of pupils who had been excluded from school were provided by staff from local FSUs and Barnardo's projects. Most (25) were male, and they covered both primary age (13) and secondary age (17). As shown below, more than half had been excluded permanently; others had been excluded indefinitely, or for a fixed term, and for some the exclusion was "informal". Nearly half were reported to have special educational needs. The families were typically on low incomes, and many had additional sources of stress.

As explained earlier, in this report we generally use "Black" to refer to people who identify themselves as of Asian, African, African-Caribbean or mixed race origin. But all the Black pupils we studied – nine out of 30 – were in fact African-Caribbean or mixed-race in origin, with the exception of one Moroccan. A summary of the cases is provided in Appendix One.

As indicated in the introduction to this report, the 30 pupils are not necessarily representative of all those excluded. Because of the nature of the work of Barnardo's and FSU projects, families often come to us for help with emotional or behavioural difficulties, or family problems of various kinds. This is likely, for example, to explain the large proportion of pupils with special educational needs among our case studies. We had also identified early on issues of concern to our two agencies which we wanted to explore, including the exclusion of younger pupils, and the disproportionate exclusion of African-Caribbean males. For this reason we asked for cases covering a spread of age and of race.

The qualitative data in this section should be seen as supplementing the statistics described earlier, and as highlighting themes which need to be addressed in future larger-scale studies. Looking in depth at 30 cases is designed to tease out some of the key issues affecting families, and to clarify the experience of exclusion from the perspective of the parent and the pupil.

The information in this chapter is provided by Barnardo's and FSU workers, and the quotations are from their case studies. It should be borne in mind that we have no information about the cases from the schools or teachers.

Key findings from the analysis of the 30 cases include:

- Some pupils were excluded for long periods with little or no educational provision.

- Most pupils had been excluded more than once, and repeated fixed-term or part-day exclusion was common.

- Parents had little information about the law on exclusion, and felt they had little power in their contact with the school.

- Workers reported that the exclusion often had a bad effect on the well-being of pupil and/or family. For a few particularly vulnerable pupils there were immediate and grave consequences.

- Most exclusions were in response to allegedly violent and/or disruptive behaviour, and a previous history of such behaviour was usually reported.

- Some parents and/or pupils felt strongly that the exclusion decision was unfair, and this may have been a particular issue for Black pupils.

- Some exclusions appeared to be directly related to the lack of, or cutbacks in, provision for special needs support.

Contact with Barnardo's, FSU and other agencies

The nature of the pupil's and family's contact with Barnardo's or FSU, and to a lesser extent the duration, was related to the specific focus and function of the project involved. Typically the Family Service Units families had been in contact some two or three years, and were receiving extensive and intensive individual and family contact, including counselling, play therapy and groupwork.

Those Barnardo's projects concerned with assessment tended to have a contact of some three to five months, and the work might also include individual counselling and other one-to-one work. Projects concerned explicitly with education maintained a longer contact time, and the association was described in terms such as "participation in full education and recreational programme."

Involvement of other agencies

The most frequently described other agencies or professionals involved with the families were the education welfare and educational psychology services. In some cases, education social workers, social services workers and/or educational psychologists were specifically said to have supported parents in dealing with the exclusion. Apart from this, the main support was obtained through Barnardo's or FSU, sometimes with other specialist assistance. And in a number of cases, no outside support appeared to have been available to parents.

The pupil's educational circumstances

Type of school

To the knowledge of the workers, none of the schools had opted out of local authority control. Four out of 11 primary schools were church schools. Details are given in Table 1.

Table 1 – Type of school

Type of school	Number
Primary	11
Middle	1
Mainstream Comprehensive	10
Mainstream Comp. with support	2
Special	4
None	1
Not given	1
Total	30

Assessment and provision for special educational needs

Just under half the pupils had received a "statement of needs", or were undergoing assessment for this. Table 2 summarises their statementing status, and also lists those pupils without statements but identified as having special educational needs .

Table 2 – Statement of special needs

Special needs	Statement	No statement
EBD*	9	3
Learning Difficulties	5	3
No SENs reported		8
Difficulty in starting statement process		2
Total	14	16

*EBD = emotional and behavioural difficulties

In two instances the child could not even gain access to a school in order to begin the process – "he cannot start because he's not attending anywhere to be assessed."

Only two out of nine Black pupils were said to have been statemented, or to be going through the process: a lower proportion than for White pupils. Chapters five and six reflect this difference in that four out of six White pupils interviewed had statements compared with only one of the Black pupils. Clearly, caution should be exercised in drawing conclusions, given the small numbers involved, and the fact that the circumstances of the pupils and families reflect the type of work and range of service users of the two agencies. But one possible implication is to support the view that exclusion affects Black pupils with less severe behaviour problems than their White counterparts (previous research has shown they are excluded for less serious offences – see chapter one). Another is that Black pupils are more likely to be seen as disruptive than as having special needs which need support (in discussion with workers in the field, the view has been expressed, though not supported unanimously, that "White pupils get statemented, Black pupils get excluded").

Of those whose special needs were reported in any detail, twelve were concerned with behaviour, and eight with learning difficulties. In both groups there were also a number of children who were said to present both behaviour and learning difficulties; in these instances the aspect which received the greater emphasis has been selected for summary purposes.

There were examples of the process being long and frustrating. A child said to be exhibiting violent or difficult behaviour could be removed from the direct attention of professionals through exclusion. There were also some professional and administrative delays, further exacerbated by the absence of provision – "....the L.E.A. offered the family an interim place of one hour per day's tutoring at an education centre in the borough."

Family and pupil at home

Family circumstances

Four pupils were in care, one attended residential special school, and two more were being cared for (partially or exclusively) by relatives.

Of the remainder, 16 lived with lone parents, and six with two parents. One boy living at home with his mother was the subject of a care order. Only one was an only child at home, and he lived with his mother.

Family income

Most of the families (23) were on income support. Others made reference to low income. In only one family was the whole family income said to be derived from employment – both mother and her partner worked, the former part-time. Another mother on income support also worked part-time.

Extra stresses

As previously mentioned, all families were receiving a service from FSU or Barnardo's and therefore many were likely to have some kind of additional stress for which they needed help. Four of the families were not recorded as having any pressures additional to the school-based one under discussion. In the remainder, a range of type and degree of stress was described, and some families were clearly under enormous pressure.

A small number of families reported *overcrowding*. The other environmental pressure was the quality of life on a housing estate –

described as "a very stressed estate", or an estate on which much joy-riding took place. A number of lone mothers were described to be suffering from stress due to *isolation:* "the stress of bringing up two children alone."

Illness and recent bereavement affected some families. For some maternal illness was the issue – the most severe example being a mother in chronic renal failure. In addition depression was a significant feature for three mothers, in two instances resulting in overdoses. Current serious illness within the family presented additional aggravation for a small number of pupils. Two of the excluded children were or had been ill themselves: one with a bronchial disorder, the other had had to undergo a series of surgical procedures because of major organ disorders. Loss of a close relative was reported in three families, and as demonstrated in chapter six, other pupils were still affected by earlier bereavements.

Given the work of Barnardo's and FSU, it would be expected that some families' contact with the agency would at least in part relate to problems caused by *domestic violence and/or sexual abuse of children.* Indeed violent behaviour by a father or other adult male was frequently recorded. Generally, but not exclusively, the mother was the victim of the assaults; in a small number of households the children were also physically abused. In addition, one father had been convicted of offences of sexual abuse. Sexual abuse was recorded as a feature in three other families.

In a small number of cases, *criminal behaviour and/or alcohol or drug misuse* were mentioned.

The pupil – views of family and worker

Many of the pupils were reported to be keen to learn and to have become proficient in several subjects – from the most practical to the most academic. For many, the principal aspiration was to be normal.

Reported relationships between pupil and family varied considerably. In a few cases these were described in close and harmonious terms, but this was sometimes overlaid with undue responsibility being placed on the pupil:

"Very helpful towards his mum, shoulders a lot of responsibility. Very loyal and protective towards her and family, has too many responsibilities."

Other responses blended positive notes with some reservations, or suggested a predisposition to being provoked easily, as in:

"Generally cheerful and friendly, but has low frustration threshold."

On the more negative side, violence and aggression (towards parent or brothers and sisters) within the home was reported frequently. In five cases no positive elements were reported, for example:

"He was demanding of mum's attention – had difficulty accepting her authority. Very aggressive towards other children – unable to share, had the ability to wind them up through name calling .... after the injury [an accident] it seems he could not cope at home, was often violent."

The exclusion

Problems before the exclusion

Whatever the incident which occasioned the exclusion in question, virtually every child described in the study was said to have presented previous problems at school of disruption or violence. There were exceptions – a child with asthma mistakenly felt to be lazy, the Muslim child at a Church of England school compelled to participate in Christian worship. The allegedly disruptive behaviour ranged from general classroom disruption to quite grave incidents of physical assault:

"....problems in school have included cheek, violent behaviour towards other pupils and an inability to abide by rules."

There was evidence that a few schools went a long way to contain the problems of pupils with severe emotional and behavioural difficulties:

"....violent outbursts, running away when in conflict .... mood swings. The school tried hard to support him, pushed for statementing. Andrew jumped out of the window."

Type and length of exclusion

The *type* of exclusion is summarised in *Table 3*

Table 3 – Type of exclusion

Permanent	17
Indefinite	7
Fixed/short term	5
Other	1

Just over half of the pupils had been *permanently* excluded from school, including two who had not been formally excluded but whose parent was asked to withdraw them. All but two had previously been excluded in some way: the permanent exclusion was often the culmination of a process involving repeated exclusions of various kinds over the preceding period. In several cases, the pupil had previously been permanently excluded from another school. Six out of nine Black pupils had been permanently excluded, of whom 1 had been withdrawn as above.

The *indefinite* exclusions lasted for anything from a few weeks to many months. As with the permanent excludees, four had previous exclusions.

Of the five *short-term* (most technically "fixed term") exclusions, two pupils were excluded for short periods of up to five days and three had repeated or continual short-term or part-day exclusions.

Repeated short-term or part-time exclusions were indeed a major feature for the pupils studied, as they had also been experienced by pupils eventually indefinitely or permanently excluded. For example Jonathan aged six had been excluded 11 times for up to three days each time, and was also sometimes sent home in the middle of the day. Several pupils attended school for half days over one or two terms at the school's request. This theme is further explored in chapter six.

James from an Irish Traveller family had not been formally excluded from an individual school, but since his arrival from Ireland three years previously, no school would accept him.

The *length* of the exclusion is summarised below in table four. When the case studies were completed, around half (15) had missed at least six months' schooling. Apart from Jonathan who had not been found a place for three years, three others had been out of school for long periods: three years, two years and 15 months respectively. At the other end of the spectrum, one pupil had only been excluded for 2 days, on each of two occasions, and another for one week.

Table 4 – Length of exclusion

Up to 1month	1-5 months	6 months – 1 year	over a year
3	12	11	4

Reason for exclusion

All of the exclusion events concerned incidents of alleged misbehaviour, rather than focusing on the specific needs of the child. For example, there was no reference to a child being excluded because of learning difficulties.

In almost all cases, the exclusion was reported to be the result of *violent, disruptive or unmanageable behaviour*, which was often said to have gone on for some time. On occasions, the issue was restricted to verbal aggression, but in some instances, the behaviour described was severe – alleged sexual attack on another pupil, or serious assaults on staff or other pupils.

As already indicated, many of the pupils had been *previously excluded* on a number of occasions and in line with this, some case studies do not describe any particular incident that triggered the current exclusion. In other cases where there was a particular incident, it seems to have been the "last straw" because of their previous history, which would not have provoked exclusion in a pupil with a different record (see Chapters five and six for more on this). The less specific the behaviour described as responsible for exclusion, the greater the likelihood of *dissent between parent or pupil and school*:

"School view – Behaviour problem, being disruptive and does not concentrate. Parent view – Darren is overweight, and is being singled out at school, victimised by school and pupils."

Such dissent was not atypical. There was also some suggestion that some school staff were more adept than others at handling difficult situations.

A number of pupils and/or their parents disputed the fairness of the exclusion because they disputed the facts of a specific incident, or felt the whole story had not come out. Sometimes the pupil, accused of violence, said they had been provoked by a fellow pupil or a teacher. For example Barry aged 11 had previously been excluded because he had injured a teacher. He was permanently excluded after he alleged a teacher had hit him: it was reported that the school would not let him return unless he retracted the allegation, which he refused to do.

In some cases, social workers, parents and/or pupils believed that a pupil with a history of difficult behaviour was *wrongly accused, scapegoated or labelled*: for example:

"Jane believes that having been identified as a troublemaker, she was not given the opportunity to be anything other."

"Mum feels it has become personalised between Dave and his head of year. ..... General terms are used e.g. "misbehaviour in class". Mum feels Dave does "talk clever" but feels he has to stick up for himself because he's Black. Dave feels the head of lower school is racist. Actual details of particular incidents are very hazy and seem a mishmash of things."

As Dave's case suggests, disputes over fairness and scapegoating/ labelling have a particular significance for *Black pupils* and chapter five explores this and related issues in greater depth.

In two cases of Black pupils, the exclusion seemed to relate to friction between parent and school. One was excluded because the school said they would not tolerate his mother's behaviour which they saw as threatening. In the other, the mother said she was told he would not be accepted back until she withdrew her allegation of racism against the headmaster.

As already discussed, over half of the pupils in this study were said to have *special educational needs, mainly emotional and behavioural difficulties.* Chapter six explores this issue in greater depth.

The lack of appropriate facilities to cope with these special needs forms a sub-text underlying a number of these exclusions. For example Peter, indefinitely excluded for six months, was subject to delays in statementing because disputes over funding responsibility between the education and social services departments meant that the "unwritten" recommendation of a residential school for pupils with emotional and behavioural disorders could not be formalised into a statement. In several other cases closure of special units or lack of classroom support seems to have been an indirect cause of exclusion. As the social worker reported in one case:

"Mother sympathised with school – could see it was a strain on teachers – but it was also a strain on daughter because she was trying to live up to expectations of school as being "normal", but she was a special needs pupil who no longer had support of [special needs] Unit. She was put in a large class and expected to cope."

Several pupils displayed extreme behaviour, including repeated violence towards other pupils or teachers and were apparently excluded because they just could not be coped with in mainstream school. For example Clark aged 11 had been out of school for three years, with the only education being provided at a Barnardo's project – though this was mainly play therapy. The social worker reports that his violent and bizarre behaviour could not be coped with in an "ordinary school". After three years an appropriate placement in a therapeutic boarding schools has still not been found. In several other cases a special school placement was eventually found, but only after a period out of school.

Parent and school

Here we provide a general picture on this, gleaned from the case studies, while Chapters 5 and 6 report directly on parents' views and experiences in greater detail.

Before the exclusion

In the majority of cases there was said to have been a high degree of parental contact with school staff before the exclusion, although relationships were not always harmonious. There were however some examples of good collaborative work, despite which a breakdown occurred:

"The mother....has worked hard with all the school including teachers, head, Education Welfare Officers, Educational Psychologist and social worker. In the first school this proved very inadequate and the mother (as well as the son) were blamed for all that happened."

On other occasions there was frequent contact of a less co-operative nature, in which, for example, the school would telephone the parent asking for the child's removal.

Contact over the exclusion

Schools nearly always *informed* parents of the exclusion, though sometimes this was not done immediately. Parents were not usually aware whether governors and LEA were informed, as should be the case in all except fixed term exclusions.

As already indicated, pupils were frequently sent home with no, or very little, *notice*: for example some were sent home during the day after a telephone call, while others arrived home at lunchtime or the end of the day with a letter saying they were henceforth excluded, or a letter arrived a few days later. This unpredictable situation could cause problems and stress at home, especially when it occurred frequently.

In a number of cases there had been *meetings* between school and parents to attempt to resolve the exclusion, though quite often these were at the parent's initiative. As described in Chapters five and six, communication with individual teachers or in meetings could often feel one-way.

Most parents were said to have little *knowledge of legal procedures* or their right to appeal (only two appeals were lodged). Even where they knew about their right to challenge exclusion, some parents were unhappy about pushing for their child to remain in a school which did not want them: eg

"Parent decided further appeal pointless as Head would be antagonistic particularly if successful."

After the exclusion

Education while excluded

Several pupils received some educational support at specialist Barnardo's projects. Otherwise, the most provided by the local education authority was said to be up to two hours per day home tuition or in a special unit: except for one pupil who received six weeks full time education at a specialist support centre which later closed.

There was a worryingly low level of provision for pupils out of school for long periods. Of the pupils who had been excluded for 6 months or more, three were said to have had no LEA input, including one 11 year old out of school for around six months whose mother paid £10 per hour from her income support for occasional private tuition. Two more had work sent home though in one case it was sent initially and not followed up. 7 others were offered home tuition ranging from a session per week to an hour a day. Three others attended Barnardo's projects.

Where pupils were sent home repeatedly, or had repeated fixed term exclusions, there appeared to have been no additional input to help them cope with the lessons they had missed.

Effects of exclusion on the pupil's education

Concerns about the educational effects of missing school were reported in most cases. Sometimes these were general, such as

"Lots of school missed therefore curriculum not covered. Dave relies on his sister for spelling."

Some pre-existent delays or learning difficulties were compounded by being out of school. More specifically, two teenagers had their preparations for GCSE or BTEC interrupted and an 11 year old suffered from lack of preparation for the move from primary to high school.

It was also considered that three pupils at a specialist Barnardo's centre attended more and achieved more than they would have done in mainstream schooling.

Exclusion and the pupil

Increasing *personal difficulties* were often associated with exclusion, though the part it played varied. For example though three pupils left the family home and were accommodated by the local authority around the period of the exclusion, in only one was a causal link with the exclusion specifically reported. However, only a minority of pupils – either with other severe personal/family traumas overshadowing the exclusion or, at the other end of the scale, only excluded briefly – seemed substantially unaffected by being excluded.

In around a quarter of the cases, there were concerns about possible or actual drifting into *petty crime, drug/solvent abuse or other dangerous behaviour*. Sometimes this seemed inevitable given their pre-existing disturbance, combined with the extra opportunities for getting into trouble while excluded. But in a few cases the fact of being excluded seemed to have played an active part. For example a boy of 14 was at risk when as a result of the exclusion his relationship with his family broke down, he slept rough for six weeks and was then accommodated by social services.

The most extreme problems were experienced by two girls aged 12 and 14, both of whom had severe emotional/behavioural difficulties resulting from childhood sexual assault. Diana was found to have been sexually abused while begging from men during the time she was excluded. For Linda aged 14 exclusion combined with the resulting rejection by her mother were profoundly upsetting. They triggered a period of acutely self-destructive behaviour involving shoplifting, drug-taking and sexual activity, in which there were fears for her physical safety and she was put on the child protection register.

In less risky cases, pupils were reported to be feeling *bored, upset and/or isolated* because of the exclusion. The most extreme of these was Clark aged 11 who had been excluded for three years:

"He is extremely angry about it, hates being a "head case". His time at home
is totally worthless, he is either locked in or roaming the street."

Some pupils felt demoralised by the exclusion, which reduced their
already *low self-esteem*. This applied to pupils of varying ages: for Barry
aged six, exclusion

"reinforces his negative image and he plays up to it."

For Matthew aged 16,

"(the) exclusion made him feel he's no chance and he was into real self-
destruct."

Exclusion and the family

For obvious reasons, the effect on the pupil and their family were
often intermeshed, and both are explored in greater detail in Chapters
five and six.

Apart from the extreme cases already described, many family
relationships were put under considerable stress. Sometimes the family
"blamed" the pupil: tensions would arise particularly where parents did
not believe their version of events. Already difficult family relationships could be exacerbated by the stigma of exclusion.

For a number of families, the major problem was having to *cope
with the child at home* all day, especially where they had serious
behaviour problems. For example, a project worker reported about a
mother's position as a consequence of the child's behaviour at home:

"He causes disturbance at home, she's being left to deal with his behaviour.
She's got the burden of what they should be coping with at school."

This situation was exacerbated where there were other family
difficulties such as a sick or disabled parent or sibling. Chapter six
explores in greater detail how parents perceived the school's
responsibility to contain their children's behaviour difficulties.

In some cases the main issue was *anxiety* about the exclusion and
about having to deal with the exclusion process, eg

"Exclusion caused his mother a great deal of worry with regard to his missed
education and the effect enforced absence from school may have on his ability
to conform in school when another placement was found."

The *effect on siblings* who became jealous and also wanted to be at home was mentioned in one or two cases. Indeed, in several families, siblings also were or had previously been excluded. For example, one pupil's two siblings were said to have drifted into total school refusal and delinquency. Some mothers with younger children had difficulty coping with the extra attention needed by the excluded pupil.

A number of families reported difficulty in managing *extra expenses* especially if the pupil was at home for long periods. These were mainly loss of free school meals, and costs of extra toys/games or occasionally outings. In several cases, there were practical problems in ensuring that the pupil was supervised safely. For example, Keith's mother found it very difficult to be frequently called away from work or college to pick him up. As indicated earlier, some older pupils were unsupervised and assessed as at risk while excluded.

The present position

In some cases there appeared to be no plans for returning to school and little or no contact with the LEA. These included some pupils who had been out of school for long periods. In other cases, plans were afoot for new placements or reintegration, but these had not yet materialised. In yet others a new placement (sometimes in a day or residential special school) appeared to be working out.

5. Interviews with Black Families

Maud Blair

This chapter reports on interviews with six Black families drawn from the 30 case studies discussed in the previous chapter, exploring key themes some of which have already been identified in that chapter. No special criteria were used for selection of the six other than the practicability of arranging to see them, and their willingness to be interviewed. Two of the pupils were of primary age, four secondary, and there were five boys and one girl. All the parents interviewed were mothers, including one foster mother; four mothers were Black and two were White. It should be noted that all the "Black" pupils in this chapter were of African-Caribbean or mixed race origin.

The following is a summary of the six cases (all names have been changed):

1 James Wilson, age 8: younger of two sons.
   Statement of special needs.
   Type of exclusion – permanent.
   Reasons for exclusion – unclear but appear to be related to hitting a disabled child. Charge denied.
   Method of exclusion – letter to parent.
   No formal 'hearing' by governors.
   Current status: Was about to start school after a year's absence.

2 Alan Christopher, age 8: only child.
   Type of exclusion – 'back door' or voluntary withdrawal.
   Reasons for exclusion – nothing specific, but continuous poor behaviour and running away from school.
   Current status: Reasonably settled in school where Headteacher made extra effort to help settle the child.

3 Nadine Philips, age 13: 4th of five children – living with her father.
Type of exclusion – permanent.
Reasons for exclusion:
– Alleged to have broken a window
– charge denied and never substantiated.
Method of exclusion – formal hearing – but parent too disillusioned to attend.
Current status – still out of school but parent pursuing local education office.

4 Andrew Langley, age 13: second of six children.
Type of exclusion – Indefinite (previously six months), currently (since beginning of terms).
Reasons for exclusion:
– smoking in school
– charge accepted but allegedly unfairly applied.
Method of exclusion – parents told to take him out, look for another school and only in the event of failing to find another school should they bring him back.
Current status – No other school found, mother reluctant to take him back to old school, child at home with unclear status and uncertain future.

5 Morris Jones, age 14: special school; fostered.
Type of exclusion – Permanent.
Reasons for exclusion – Originally rape – denied and disproved. Finally, alleged bullying. Charge denied.
Method of exclusion – bus pass taken away, letter written, no formal 'hearing' to foster parent's understanding.
Current status – still uncertain after a year, waiting to hear from social worker who was on holiday at time of interview.

6 Demian Andrews, age 14: second of three sons; father has other children who live with their own mother, father not at home – possibly in prison.
Type of exclusion – Permanent.
Reasons for exclusion – stabbing another boy in the arm; method – formal hearing – parent too disillusioned to attend.
Current status – in secure unit for juveniles.

The analysis below is based entirely on interview discussions held with these pupils and their mothers during September and October 1993. All pupils listed were, at the time of the interview, excluded (four permanently) from their schools and still awaiting decisions about the new placements. One pupil was not living at home, but in a secure unit for juveniles.

The material will be organised into four sections:

The first section will focus on the type and reasons for the exclusions and the procedures used in the various schools to exclude the pupil. As the reasons differ from pupil to pupil, and the procedures vary from one school to another, it will be necessary to outline these differences in order to convey the lack of consistency in cases of pupil exclusion.

The second section will look at in-school processes which might contribute to the conditions which lead to pupil exclusions. It is important to underline that the views conveyed are those of pupils and their parents only and that it was not the purpose of this study to seek the views of teachers or education officials. General conclusions will be drawn from the views of the two groups of parents and pupils and individual comments will be quoted only to illustrate a general point which is relevant to or is illustrative to the experiences of all the families.

The third section will look at the effects of the school processes and the exclusion, on the family lives of the respondents. Again, a general analysis will be made except where individual family experiences differ so drastically from the others as to make a special focus necessary.

The conclusion and final section will attempt to summarise the salient points which underline both the educational and family implications for the respondents.

Exclusions

Types of exclusions

Although four of the pupils had been permanently excluded from their schools, all had experienced other forms of exclusion both formal and informal. The most common was the 'Corridor' exclusion whereby pupils (whether primary or secondary) who misbehave or cause disruption are banished to stand outside the classroom door or outside the headteacher's office (or other person of higher status than the classroom teacher) for the duration of the lesson. They usually rejoin their peers at the end of the particular session. The second was the 'withdrawal room' which is a room especially set aside to place such pupils. This too is usually for the duration of the lesson after which pupils rejoin their class. These are informal methods of exclusion commonly used in schools and can but do not necessarily lead to a formal exclusion. All the pupils in the study had experienced this form of exclusion, which had implications for those subject areas where interactions between particular teachers and pupils meant that the pupils were regularly missing out on the lesson in question. This could contribute to a cycle of underachievement which then led to further disaffection and strained pupil/teacher relationships. This was a concern of one of the parents who indicated that her son who was still in primary school, seemed to spend more time in the corridor than in the classroom.

Formal exclusions included fixed term exclusions, which for these pupils had ranged from two days to two weeks, and indefinite. One of the pupils had waited six months to return to school after the first indefinite exclusion and was on his second indefinite exclusion which at the time of the interview had reached three weeks. As on both occasions the pupil had been excluded indefinitely very shortly after the beginning of the new academic year, the parent concluded cynically that her son was kept on the books and not permanently excluded in order to ensure that funding for him continued to come to the school.

A permanent exclusion meant that a pupil could not return to the school and was formally removed from the register. A further 'unofficial' category of exclusion has been used by schools to replace the permanent exclusion but have the same effect. This has been termed the 'backdoor' exclusion because parents are told to remove their children voluntarily from the school and avoid the stigma of a formal exclusion, thereby easing the pupil's transfer to another school. In practice, this did not always have the desired effect as one of the parents explained. She had been put under pressure to remove her child but discovered that finding another school was still far from easy. The main obstacle, it was felt, was the 'Headteacher grapevine' by which the Headteacher of a potential new school was briefed about the child's history by the previous Head and was likely to reject the pupil on that basis. Indeed, this particular parent's situation was made worse because by withdrawing her child she had forfeited the right to official help from the local education authority. Her lack of information of schools in the area and her reticence to deal with headteachers thus made the task a particularly difficult one for her. In fact, it is considered inadvisable for a child with a special needs statement to voluntarily withdraw from the school as this could mean that the pupil was no longer entitled to whatever educational benefits might be gained from having a statement.

Reasons for exclusion

The most serious reasons for exclusion in this case study were allegations of rape and stabbing. Other reasons ranged from continuous reports of misbehaviour, hitting a disabled pupil, smoking on the school premises and breaking a window. The rape, stabbing, breaking a window and hitting a disabled pupil were never substantiated and all but the stabbing were vigorously denied by the pupils concerned. The boy in the rape case returned to school after medical examination of the girl showed no sign of sexual molestation, but the boy was soon after excluded permanently for alleged bullying – an accusation which he also denied. It is possible that the school needed to find reasons to let him go when the mother of the girl refused to bring her daughter back to the school as long as the boy remained. The boy admitted to poor relations with one of the teachers, a situation which could not have helped his case.

One boy admitted to stabbing another pupil in the arm during a fight. It was difficult to ascertain the truth of his admission to the stabbing as the boy seemed to weave a web of fantasy around himself on a number of issues. Although the stabbing was never proved, and the boy had at the time denied the allegation, he was nevertheless excluded. His major grievance against the school was that the fight in which he was involved was the result of a long period of intimidation on the part of the other boy. The intimidation was never investigated, neither was he invited to present his side of the story. This was a general complaint made by the other pupils in the study.

The broken window was also never proved. It would seem that although a dinner supervisor had vouched for the girl's presence at dinner at the time of the incident, this was not taken into account by the school. According to the mother, her daughter had been in trouble in the school so many times because of her attitude to school, that it was possible that the school were waiting for just such an opportunity to exclude her.

The boy alleged to have hit a disabled pupil claimed that although the boy had cried, he had not meant to hurt him as it had happened in play. The mother also said that she had investigated the claim of serious bruising of the disabled boy's back but that this boy's parents had not found any such bruising.

Although the pupils did not deny that they often got into trouble at school, the final reasons for permanent exclusion of the pupils concerned had left a deep sense of injustice in them and their parents. The fact that the cases were never proved, and the fact that other pupils who became involved in fights or smoking were not excluded, strengthened the overall feeling that the schools concerned no longer wanted these pupils and had found the first excuse to get rid of them. This sense of distrust was compounded by the absence of proper procedures or the haphazard approach taken by individual schools to the exclusion of these pupils. This is the subject of the next section.

Exclusion procedures

In only two of the cases were proper exclusion procedures followed. But the fear of victimisation in one form or another of their children convinced parents the appeals system would not work in their favour. Not only did they feel that they were unlikely to win an appeal, but to appeal was merely to invite the whole cycle of problems if the children were to be returned to the same schools which had excluded them.

In two cases, the parents had not been informed of procedures and only learnt, by letter, that their children were not to return to school. In another case, the parent had been pressured into withdrawing her son only to find that the Education Welfare Officer who had been helping her could not continue as her son was no longer an 'official' case. Another boy was suspended on a semi-permanent 'indefinite' exclusion. In this case, the school had advised the parents to find a place elsewhere, and return if they did not succeed. However, when they tried different schools in the area, they found that the child's reputation had preceded him along the Headteacher grapevine and none of the local schools had been prepared to take him. On the other hand, the Headteacher of his current school had made it so clear that she did not want him back, that to take him back to the same school was to return to the merry-go-round of trouble followed by exclusion which was causing so much stress and anxiety to the family. Yet the Headteacher would not permanently exclude, a procedure which would effectively place the responsibility for the pupil's placement into the hands of the local education office who could force a school with space to take him. The child, therefore, remained suspended in limbo.

Of the two cases where proper procedures had been followed, the parents concerned expressed a sense of deep disillusionment with the system which they felt was weighted so heavily against them that to attend an exclusion 'hearing' was not only a waste of their time and energy but was likely to have further negative effects on their already battered emotions. Such decision, they felt, would invariably go in favour of the Headteacher as experience with other children had shown.

In-school processes

Pupils and teachers

Out of the six pupils, one attended a school for children with learning difficulties and one had a statement of special needs. All the pupils stressed that they liked school and were happy at school. The boy in the secure unit particularly regretted not being able to attend a mainstream school.

They all admitted that they did get into trouble at school, but thought that most of the things they did were 'normal' for pupils of their ages. Two main themes emerged from the interviews. The first was the feeling (and at times the certainty) that they were treated *unfairly*. They were unclear about the reasons for this and by and large felt that the colour of the teacher was not always an important factor although none of them had ever taught by a Black teacher. But not all White teachers treated them unfairly and individual White teachers had been particularly good to them. The older pupils were, nevertheless, puzzled by their own observations that in the schools which they had attended, it was mainly the Black pupils who seemed to get into the most trouble. Some White teachers were singled out as racist and it was with these teachers that pupils got into the most trouble. For example, one pupil who was one of a small minority of Black pupils in the school described how the Headteacher 'freaked' when she saw that he was Black. The Headteacher had until then only met his mother who was White. The mother in turn talked about her feeling that the Headteacher held her in contempt, treated her dismissively and was inclined to single her son out unfairly.

At this point it is important to acknowledge that while parents' and pupils' individualised perceptions and experiences led them to focus on racism by particular teachers and pupils, all the processes of exclusion affecting the cases studied pointed to wider institutional practices confirming the effects of institutional racism.

The second theme was that teachers never *listened* to their point of view. In a conflict between two pupils, for example, teachers only seemed to see the retaliatory response of the (Black) pupil and seemed uninterested to investigate some of the invisible forms of intimidation such as racist name-calling to which Black pupils were subject.

"They never ever listened to me. Every time I go to a teacher and say 'look sir, he's doing this and that', they're not interested in listening to me. They won't listen to me, they don't want to listen to me. They won't listen to pupils anyway."

That racist name-calling had a profound impact on the pupils was quite clear. When one pupil was asked how high on the list he would put racist name-calling out of the things that made him angry, he replied without hesitation, 'TOP'.

But there was a sense that teachers were insensitive to this and were unsupportive or else showed some sympathy and encouraged the pupils to report such incidents and then nothing was done. One eight year old who suffered from obesity and was the butt of much teasing and intimidation said that he sometimes took matters into his own hands because although the teacher had told him to put his hand up to report such incidents when they occurred in the classroom, when he did put his hand up the teacher ignored him. One mother reported:

"...Everyday he kept calling her (names). She knew she shouldn't, she said to me 'I shouldn't have kicked him, I know I shouldn't, but what am I to do. No-one don't do anything."

Sometimes teachers made unkind remarks which led to confrontations with pupils. The same eight year old who suffered from obesity had been terrified to go to school because the dinner supervisor had threatened to "prick him with a pin until he popped".

The overall conclusion therefore was that pupils acquired reputations as 'bad' characters through their interactions with certain teachers who were either racist or with whom they simply 'did not get on'. Sometimes this reputation carried over from primary school into the secondary school through the usual report system used by headteachers. But having acquired such a reputation, they were then closely watched by the school as a whole and were likely to be blamed for things they had not done, and reprimanded or punished more severely than others who might be involved in the same or similar activities, the assumption being that they needed to be controlled more firmly than others.

This resulted in a sense of grievance about unfair treatment and unjust punishment which was compounded by the belief that teachers were not interested in listening to different points of view and to take account of events which caused conflicts to arise.

Parents' views

Teacher attitude was seen by the parents as the most damaging cause of poor or deteriorating relations between parents and the school, and a contributory factor to the problems that pupils faced. A number of common themes appeared.

Unfair treatment

All the parents talked about their inability to help change their own children's attitudes to school in the context of negative teacher attitudes to pupils. That pupils were not given the opportunity to make a fresh start when they moved from one school to another, was seen as iniquitous. Pupils' reputations preceded them to their new schools so that teachers operated with preconceptions thus condemning them to a permanent 'loser' category which had its own self-fulfilling effects.

"...he seems to settle down, and he can have good times, and then it'll just, I don't know, he seems to get one teacher that says, 'we know all about you', and it starts all over again."

All the parents reinforced the view that having got labelled, the pupil was less likely to experience fair treatment and was likely to be 'picked on' and blamed more than others.

"She just has to see a little crowd and (my son) be in it, she'd be taking him out, and not knowing what's going on but just taking him out."

Furthermore, this labelling did not stop with the pupil in question but was extended to his/her siblings which tended to establish a 'family' rather than an individual reputation, with unfortunate consequences.

"She compares my other two daughters to him all the time. She pulls them all the time in the corridor about his behaviour – So now, both of them, it's no longer, they're in school, but it's 'can I have a day off and I don't feel well' and it's because they know she's going to teach them and she's going to compare them all the time and it's not right."

As shown in chapter four and six, such 'labelling' of pupils was also reported in other cases.

Teachers' attitudes to pupils

For some pupils, labelling meant that their good and positive points were never realised and therefore never nurtured, fostering a sense of doom in the parents.

"Mrs M really did try with Rachel. She praised her and encouraged her and Rachel is doing quite well – that's until they break her down. I shouldn't say that when she's listening to me but I'm waiting for it, they've got a new teacher."

In another situation, a teacher who had taken it upon herself to spend extra time and effort encouraging a pupil and communicating regularly with the parent had stopped when her reports of the pupil's progress conflicted with the reports which came from the Headteacher. Whatever the reasons for this occurrence, it reinforced the feeling that parents and pupils would always be losers because teachers 'stuck together'. Parents felt that their children had positive points and talents which if only teachers took the trouble to nurture, might lead to more rewarding experiences of school for them. Instead it was felt that teachers showed little interest and respect for the pupils sense of self.

"I don't feel there's anything I can do. I mean, how can I stop the teacher talking to him the way they do, you know. I can't say well if you talk to (my son) properly, he'll talk to you properly. You treat him with a bit of respect, he'll treat you with a bit of respect. I can't, you know, because to me the school will say, 'well it's not us, it's your son, the problem's him, not us'."

Reports on pupils

Parents generally felt that they received conflicting reports about their children depending on the teacher. For example a pupil might be described by one teacher as a bully whilst another would say how helpful and kind the pupil was to others. Some parents were concerned that such reports invariably focused on the child's behaviour and said little about the child's academic progress. The parents of the two primary school pupils expressed particular concern about positive reports teachers made of their children's academic progress when their children still could not read very basic words. What they wanted was an honest representation of their children's progress both behavioural and academic and not a report which they felt was designed to encourage parents to control their children's behaviour whilst keeping them ignorant of their children's actual academic progress.

Racism

Apart from one parent who felt anger against all White people, all the others went out of their way to stress that the racism their children experienced was a factor of individual behaviour, but they *all* believed that it played a part in their children's experiences of school. One White parent felt that racism was a component in one headteacher's attitude towards her because she had been married to a Black man. Like the other parents, she thought that Black pupils were often blamed for things they did not do, not only by teachers, but by other pupils. One parent gave this example:

"Only last night, Rachel came back and said that a little girl in her class, Zoe, told her mum outside the school that she had pushed her and she actually eat her words in the end this mum because it was somebody else that pushed her."

The same woman gave an example of her son being blamed for taking money from a younger child when it was later discovered that he had actually been actively preventing another boy from taking the money. He had nevertheless been identified to the police as the one who had taken the money.

Racist name-calling was a common experience for Black pupils. By and large the grievance was against teachers who did not take a stand on the matter rather than on the pupils who indulged this kind of behaviour. It was felt that both in this matter and in all other forms of behaviour, pupils were not given secure boundaries which helped them to understand what was acceptable and what was not.

Teacher-parent relationships

A strong theme to emerge in this area was the sense of *parental powerlessness* against education officials, headteachers and teachers; this theme is also echoed in Chapter six.

Like their children, the mothers felt that they were not listened to and that there was nothing they could do about it. A few quotes will illustrate this.

"Oh yeah, they sit you down and listen but at the end of the day they say whatever they wanted to."

"I didn't try to phone (another school) because they are not going to listen. They listen to what me say, yes, but what the other headmistress say much more for listen than what me tell them, so I didn't waste my time. I don't know. You at the mercy of these people – You have to abide by what they do or otherwise you like it or lump it."

"Nobody listens to me when I say I'd prefer (my son) somewhere where I know he's getting an education and I know there's not going to be writing to me all the time, you know. That is all I've asked for."

The sense of powerlessness was compounded for the parents by the feeling of alienation from official discourse and the inconsistency of the support (if any) which they received or had been promised by the local education office. Officials were said to backtrack on their promises, or to make offers of help which they never followed up, to give up help when a parent or child most needed it or simply not to communicate with the parent about whatever progress was being made about their child's education. There was a sense of hopelessness because of lack of access to information which would help them to be less dependent on others to get things done. As a result, some pupils had been out of school for the best part of an academic year and the parents were still unsure as to what to do.

"It would be very nice if I could get somebody who knows the rights and wrongs and knows what my options are for (my son), where he can go or what we can do because at the moment, I don't even know in which direction to go to because I've been in them all so until somebody comes to me and says well, he could go here, you know."

But even if they did make contact with someone who was in a position to help them, they did not necessarily make any progress:

"Everyone that you go to ask to forward you onto the right person to go and make a complaint, nobody don't give no leeway. I'm still waiting on the education inspector to get back in touch with me for tell me whether or not (the headmistress) take the right procedure and up to now she never get back to me."

Officials' attitudes to parents

Associated with the sense of powerlessness, being 'shut out', and not having any control over their lives and their children's lives, was a sense that officialdom or the middleclass world of school staffrooms treated them with disrespect if not outright contempt. This is what one parent had to say about the Deputy Headteacher.

"Because when I'm speaking to her, she would just dismiss things, she wouldn't talk to me like I was somebody. Like, if I say, 'what happened, what did you do, how did you handle it', you know, she wouldn't talk to me properly – I suggested things and we had so much arguments because in the end I just couldn't talk to her. I just thought she didn't have no manners, she didn't have no respect for me as a person, she just dismissed me when she was talking to me."

Often, this could lead to a serious breakdown in communication which became part of a spiral of misunderstanding, misinformation and mutual distrust. One parent was sure that the Headteacher had excluded her child in order to get back at her for not agreeing with the official line at a meeting. Another was suspicious of a contract she was asked to sign which she felt was entirely on the headteacher's terms and did not adequately represent her child's interests. The White parents suspected – though as one of them said, it was difficult to prove – that part of official treatment of them stemmed from the fact that they had been married to Black men. One Black woman's experiences with the police and other white officials outside the education context had made her very distrustful of all White officials, including teachers. Her own experiences as a pupil in school in Britain had convinced her of the need to intervene on behalf of her children whenever they were treated unfairly or racially abused. Needless to say this led to many conflicts particularly with those teachers whose actions she felt were underpinned by racism.

The effects of exclusion on the lives of respondent families

The effects of exclusion were felt well before the actual event in the build up of conflict and the deteriorating relations between the parents and the schools. The final exclusion of the pupil therefore needs to be seen in this context and in the context of the pupil's home circumstances.

Home circumstances

All the families interviewed were either on income support or in low income brackets. The larger families lived in over-crowded conditions which were already a source of stress. One mother who lived with her partner and six children in a three bedroomed house had to go to work because they would otherwise not be able to make ends meet. She worked mornings in order to enable her to be home in the afternoons when the children returned from school. Her son at thirteen wanted some space to himself but had to share his bedroom with two younger brothers. Another parent in similar conditions had grown increasingly concerned about her daughter coming home after dark from visiting her friends especially in an area known for racial attacks and murders of Black people.

"It got to she wasn't coming home till eleven o'clock at night and I had four others to look after and looking for her out on the streets at night time was just totally, oh devastating to the whole family because (the others) were bringing me work home and I couldn't even think..."

These conditions of poverty, overcrowding, and racial tension formed some of the background to children's lives in school. The unhelpfulness of education officials, the attitudes of teachers and headteachers and sometimes the absence of anyone to turn to for help could only add to what were sometimes already very stressful situations.

Emotional Stress

"My older daughter was also having difficulties at her school and then when (my son) started it got very difficult for me because I was running in between two schools, work, having a baby, you know, and trying to sort out all these things all at the same time and I just didn't know whether I was coming or going, it was really really difficult."

Her son's indefinite exclusion did not ease the situation as officially it was not known that he was out of school. She now had to start 'running around' in another direction trying to find help to sort out his education and coming upon brick walls. Her partner did not like the boy to be at home all the time, and yet she could not let him wander the streets without having some control over his whereabouts. She feared that he might get involved in petty crime, or be the target of police surveillance.

".. basically, the police have even told me, it's because he is the only half-caste and he is with a load of White lads they only see the one because he is the different one from the rest, do you know what I mean, he is the one half-caste lad and like, he sticks out because..."

The foster mother of a boy with learning difficulties described the stress that his exclusion had caused both to him and her.

"I said are they going to find a school for him or send him to some centre because we can't have a 15 year old boy trailing behind us. Wherever you go he have to go because they're saying to you, you can't leave him on his own – I go into the doctor, he's behind me, I'm going to the optician, he's behind me..."

Effects of exclusion on pupils

Some of the pupils had already spent long periods of time out of school. They were all very bored and spent most of their time watching television. The foster parents of the boy with learning difficulties took him out for walks to relieve his boredom. They also gave him little tasks to perform and some writing, but as the mother said in frustration "...he can't read, he can't write and it's just a shambles".

The mother of the boy who suffered from obesity was worried because the ready access to food and the long empty hours without exercise were not helping his condition. Parents were worried about their children's involvement in crime and also that they were falling so far behind their peers in school. Two of the pupils had been given work to do at home, but little care had been taken to make it meaningful.

"What I got was a photostatted bunch of papers which she'd done before, of work to do. That's it. No-one ever asked about work to be taken back or to be marked or anything. It was just photostatted pieces of paper."

"She eventually sent work home for him. But then nobody come to pick it back up and there wasn't anything on it that was saying what to do or anything. It were just a book, paper and that was it, nothing, no set work."

Effects on families

Although the events which lead up to an exclusion cause families a lot of stress, the uncertainty and anxiety experienced by parents as a result of exclusion, and the boredom of the child combine to create conditions which strain the relationships within the families themselves.

"I think I'm just getting sorted out, back to square one again, you know, he's out of school, which is very difficult for me and my partner because I don't agree for half the things he's getting kicked out for. My partner doesn't like him in all the time. But he gets bored. He gets ratty, he just gets everyone's backs up all the time because he's bored, there's nothing to do – Because of all this, we're getting at him all the time because they're getting at us, the other kids are getting at us because they feel he's getting away with, so we're constantly getting at him and he feels that he's in the wrong no matter what he does or says and he feels that I'm agreeing with the teachers and, you know, with the school, so therefore he gets his back up, there's arguments here, there's arguments there, and he's feeling he's getting owt from anybody so, you know, it's very difficult for us, very difficult."

The families also feel the financial burden of having someone at home all the time. Not only do they have to have more food in the home, but some occasions call for 'babysitters'. Indefinite exclusions create the added burden of families having to continue to buy school uniforms as the child grows and the family wait for him/her to be recalled to school.

Conclusion

From the analysis above, it seems clear that the exclusion of a pupil from school can cause enormous mental and emotional stress to the families concerned. Problems can sometimes occur a long time before the final indefinite or permanent exclusion whilst the exclusion itself brings with it a new set of difficulties and traumas.

It appears that the conditions for an exclusion do not lie exclusively within the home or the school, neither are they solely the result of pathological behaviour on the part of the pupil. The parents and pupils interviewed freely admitted that rules were sometimes broken and punishment was often deserved. But the inconsistent application of rules, the absence of clear and fair boundaries for pupils, together with a complex interaction of poverty, 'race', and class, (and presumably gender if one looks at the national statistics for boys and girls who are excluded), seem to create fertile ground for conflict within the institution of the school.

From the perspective of the parents and the pupils, conflict could be reduced if teachers listened more and tried to respect the views of pupils and in particular of the parents. The sense of being treated like a nobody or with contempt was one about which parents felt particularly aggrieved. Pupils also needed to feel respected, and importantly to be seen as people with potential both academically and socially. The tendency to undermine any potential for change that a pupil might have by categorising them permanently as troublemakers without taking into account changing circumstances was condemned by all who took part in the study. It was felt that this led to a self-fulfilling prophecy of disillusionment and loss of faith in the system, which could only encourage further bad behaviour and exacerbate poor relations. When racism either underpinned or was an added ingredient to this situation, it created conditions in which Black pupils felt particularly vulnerable and therefore more likely to become disaffected.

The abuse of the exclusions system by some schools had led to some pupils falling out or disappearing from the system altogether, whilst the long periods of waiting for those still in the system creates even more problems for those families who, like the families in the study, already experienced stressful socio-economic conditions. Despite the difficulties, the parents interviewed continued to struggle for the educational rights of their children. Sometimes the sense of powerlessness was overwhelming as one woman declared:

"They punish children when they've been naughty by kicking them out of school, right, because that's their punishment. But when they do an injustice, who parents go to for deal with them. Who, who does parents go to deal with them..?"

But at the same time, the struggle to take some control of their lives did not diminish. For one woman however, it meant abandoning her own class position and adopting the terms that 'professionals' dictated

– an option only open to those who could take time out to learn about the system and gather the kind of 'cultural capital' which enabled them to communicate with professionals on an equal basis.

"...it's just that I had to stop being a frustrated angry mother and be on a professional level, just like they are, you know. It's something that you just say as a mother, 'that's it, you're not taking no more rubbish, you know. It's about time you make the decisions for your child and, you know, for you. And that's what I did and I wasn't taking their rubbish no more and I wasn't listening to their rubbish no more and I think that helps as well, I really do."

6. Interviews with White Families

Introduction

Interviews with six White families were carried out in September and October 1993. Five out of five excluded pupils were boys. Two were of primary school age and four secondary. Four mothers and one couple were interviewed; we were unable to interview the mother of one pupil. We interviewed five of the six pupils. As with chapter five, this chapter conveys the views of pupils and parents only.

Three of the six pupils had been permanently excluded, one had been excluded indefinitely and the other two had been excluded for short periods ("fixed term") or on an informal basis only. Three had been successfully placed in a new school or college by the time we interviewed them.

As with the Black families, interviewees were selected from among the cases studied on the sole basis of their willingness to talk to us and the practicability of arranging the interviews. Four out of six had statements of special educational needs, another had received a general assessment from the Educational Psychologist and the last had received special needs support. All were said to have emotional/ behavioural problems and some also learning difficulties. Three pupils were at special schools when interviewed. So this part of the report deals primarily with pupils with special needs – as discussed earlier, these are a large proportion of the cases studied.

A summary of the cases follows; as with chapters four and five, all names have been changed.

1 Roger Collins, aged 9: only child, mother interviewed.
  Statement of special educational needs.

Type of exclusion: repeated fixed term and informal part-day or full day.

No alternative education.

Reason for exclusion: difficult behaviour. Regularly informally excluded on the day if special needs teacher or classroom helper not available, mother often phoned to fetch him home.

Currently successfully placed in day special school.

2 Andrew Smith, aged 13: oldest of three children.

Statement of special educational needs.

Type and length of exclusion: permanent. Subsequently excluded from off-site special education unit where attended part-time for a brief period – no other alternative education.

Reason for exclusion: allegedly pulling a knife which he and mother deny.

Exclusion took place very soon after placed in comprehensive following primary education in boarding special school.

Length of exclusion: most of a school year, only provision a brief period in special unit (see above).

Method of exclusion: mother invited to meeting at school but unable to attend. Currently attending residential special school where placed a year after exclusion from comprehensive.

3 Anne Linden, aged 15: in care, Barnardo's worker also interviewed.

Statement of special educational needs.

Type of exclusion:

a) permanent summer 1991 after on-site special unit closed,

b) after new school placement, a number of fixed-term and in-school exclusions, then permanent February 1993. Only education supplied by Barnardo's and working on her own.

Reason for exclusion: most recently, swearing at a teacher.

Length of exclusion: most recent exclusion, 6 months.

Current status: attending GCSE course at further education college (special dispensation); assessed to take GCSEs after one year's study.

4 Donald Bishop, aged 11: older of two children.

No statement although received an assessment from psychologist.

Type of exclusion: several fixed term or part day (including dinner-breaks) leading up to indefinite.

Length: six months indefinite exclusion. Offered two hours tuition per day at school/unit for children with learning difficulties, although his intelligence is assessed as above average.
Reason for exclusion: fighting and disruption.
Current status: following grandmother approaching the head of another comprehensive, against the advice of education officials, Donald successfully placed. Head teacher seems to be making special efforts.

5 Martin Davis, aged 15: oldest of 5 siblings, one in care, Martin currently living away from home.
Statement of special educational needs, placed at residential special school.
Type of exclusion: a number of fixed term exclusions culminating in permanent exclusion when in mainstream school. At special school also some fixed term exclusions.
Length: several months' permanent exclusion between mainstream and special school, plus many short periods. Also truants.
Reason for exclusion: disruption and (most commonly) fighting.
Current status: truanting (he says because wanted by the police).

6 Michael Thomas, aged 11: oldest of three children, baby sister seriously ill.
No statement but parents want one; received extra help in primary school.
Type of exclusion: repeated informal and/or fixed term, then indefinite half day from middle school. Placed in high school September, already fixed term exclusions when interviewed October.
Length: two terms half day exclusions, plus various formal/fixed term.
Reasons for exclusion: alleged unmanageable behaviour.
Current status: parents unsure but think fixed term exclusion.

The exclusions

Types of exclusion

Formal or informal exclusion was a regular feature of school life for some of these pupils. Most had undergone a variety of types of exclusion, including being out of school for short periods or parts of days as well as, for some, formal indefinite or permanent exclusion.

Anne, Andrew and Martin had been permanently excluded from more than one school.

As with the Black pupils, 'within school' exclusion from lessons or at dinner breaks was mentioned. For example Anne said that at one time she was excluded from much of the mainstream curriculum because of a conflict with a particular teacher. She had to stand outside the classroom for the whole lesson, or go to a special unit for most of the day which other pupils only attended for limited periods.

Reasons for exclusion

These mirrored the reasons described in Chapter four: they were generally excluded for alleged disruptive behaviour, unmanageability in the classroom or fighting. A number of issues emerged.

Some exclusions appeared to be directly linked with a *lack of appropriate provision* for pupils needing individual support. This was overt in the case of Roger, who was sent home when special needs staff were not around. His mother explained:

"...through cuts and everything it [on-site unit] started stopping and if Alison [unit teacher] weren't there, she were off sick or something, helper weren't there or something, then Roger had to come back..."

Similarly Anne's social worker saw her second exclusion mainly as a result of changes in the provision of special needs support in the LEA area, involving the closure of on-site units to support pupils with behavioural difficulties. Michael's parents said they valued the small group support which he received in primary school, and thought he subsequently got into trouble partly because this was not available in middle school.

Sometimes there was a dispute about the *fairness* of the decision to exclude, in terms of a specific incident on which the decision was based. For example Andrew was excluded after a very short time at mainstream school because he was alleged to have pulled a knife, though he and his mother said it was a pair of nail-clippers. Andrew said that he did not get the opportunity to talk to the teachers about this. Ms. Smith, while acknowledging his behavioural difficulties, also felt the decision was unfair. She thought the school were on the lookout for trouble with Andrew as they had been reluctant to take him. This issue of labelling also came up more generally in relation to school processes, as discussed below.

In general, the permanent exclusions reflected *ongoing difficulties* in containing the pupil rather than one-off serious incidents. Thus Anne was excluded permanently for swearing at a teacher but this was only the culmination of a series of incidents between them. Where accusations of misbehaviour were general, they were difficult to deal with or to challenge. Michael's parents complained:

"We're in the dark with that school, we just don't know what's going on. There's a letter home about his behaviour but they don't explain about his behaviour....They don't say whether he's been cheeky to the teacher or whether he's stamped his feet or whether he swore at them or anything."

Exclusion procedures

From the families' perspective, these were confusing, and often highly informal; it was not always evident that legal requirements had been followed. There were numerous instances of pupils being sent home after, at most, a phone call. For example Roger's mother only received one letter about an exclusion, even though he was sent home many times.

Letters informing about exclusion sometimes arrived days after the exclusion had started. And while such letters may have fulfilled legal requirements they left most parents feeling in the dark and unaware of their rights. For example the letter to Michael's parents did not say how long his afternoon exclusion would continue, and it only ended when an education welfare officer made enquiries on their behalf.

Because of parents' lack of knowledge about the procedure surrounding exclusion it was often difficult to find out from them exactly what procedures had been used, for example whether meetings they had attended at the school had been part of the formal exclusion process. Ms. Bishop spoke for the majority:

"...I didn't know what to think, I didn't know the system or anything....no-one sits down and says oh, A, B, and C, you should do this or you should do that. I didn't know."

Only one mother appeared to be fully aware that there might be a right of appeal against exclusion, though she did not think it worth taking up. Others were in the position of Mr Thomas:

....we don't know what's the law or how long they can actually keep him out of school."

Furthermore in several instances, the first the pupil knew of the exclusion was a letter arriving at home.

Two families had been involved in, or invited to, what appeared to be formal meetings at the school as part of the exclusion process. Ms. Smith's invitation to the meeting to discuss Andrew's permanent exclusion arrived on the day of the meeting. She could not go because there wasn't enough time to arrange care for her younger children.

Martin and his mother had been to a number of meetings, some involving social services but others appearing to be about truancy and/or exclusion. Martin said that he "didn't understand a word" and amplified:

"...I couldn't get a word in. They were just saying, oh, you have to do this and you have to do that."

Clearly, the nominal right to attend a meeting is not always enough.

Martin's situation underlines the pupil's lack of rights in the exclusion process. Anne came up against this forcibly when she wrote to Social Services asking if she could use the Children Act provisions to appeal against her own exclusion. They replied that as she was in care "voluntarily" her natural mother would have to appeal, which she refused to do. Anne was angry:

"...my mum hasn't known me since I was 11 but she can still say what I can do and what I can't do."

Processes at school

Positives about school

Most of the pupils said they wanted to be at school and expressed particular interest in one or more school subjects. In Anne's case this extended to working systematically on her own in the public library, encouraged by her foster mother, for several months while excluded.

Although the exclusion(s) had involved conflicts with the school, each child interviewed spoke favourably of some teachers and/or of previous schools. A recurring theme was that they liked teachers to take time to listen and discuss with them. For example Michael aged 11 contrasted his favourite teacher (who worked with a small group) with others:

"He's nice, he doesn't shout at you...he sits down, he explains things to you."

Pupils with emotional/behavioural difficulties may need even more than others to feel listened to and acknowledged in an unhurried way.

Dealing with conflict: pupils' views

As with the Black pupils, those interviewed did not generally deny they had been involved in misbehaviour. But they did sometimes think they were blamed unfairly for particular incidents. It was especially easy for teachers to label a pupil with a reputation for disruption, so (s)he was always seen as responsible for trouble. Martin felt this happened to him. When he first went to his special school both he and the other party to any fight would be excluded (fixed term): but over the last year it would just be him. Yet because he was known as the "hardest" boy in the school, others saw him as a challenge:

"Sometimes someone'd pick a fight with me and the teacher didn't see that, the teacher just saw me hitting them...I've always got a reputation for it."

Anne felt she was similarly labelled at her school, partly because of the bad reputation of an older sibling.

When involved in a specific incident leading to exclusion, pupils generally felt they had insufficient opportunity to put their side of the story or to discuss the decision to exclude: as shown by the fact that they did not always know they had been excluded.

Older pupils were clear that *discussion was needed* to clarify the responsibility for the triggering incident, or to defuse a row with a teacher. What was termed disruptive behaviour by the school might be seen by the pupil as a row between two individuals. For example Anne said that at her second school it was always one teacher she got into trouble with, and was prepared to accept some share of the responsibility for their frequent clashes: "I could be a bit of a cow". She suggested that the situation should have been resolved by a

"separate meeting, like he has one meeting with the governor and I sit down and chat to the same one and they write it down and then see what the problem is, why we didn't get on."

Ms. Bishop was impressed by the head of Donald's new school, who defused a stand-up row between him and a teacher by talking separately to all concerned and then negotiating a contract.

There were several complaints about individual teachers' *lack of respect* in the approach to pupils, including use of physical punishment or shouting. Michael aged 11 had been very distressed by being slapped by a teacher, and described other teachers shouting routinely. When he was accused of bad behaviour in the classroom, this was the response from two senior teachers to whom he was sent:

"So I went down to Ms. X, she shouted at me, and she said I'm going to give you a letter at home time, then she sent me back to Mr Y, Mr Y shouted in my ear so I run off."

Michael thought the worst thing about teachers was

"Shouting in your ear...yeah, really close, makes you jump and cry."

Parents' contact with the school and educational authorities.

General

In different ways and to different degrees, all the parents expressed a strong feeling of having to struggle against *powerlessness* in relation to the education system. This echoed the views of Black parents discussed in chapter five, but the elements of that powerlessness do seem to differ.

These parents all saw their children as presenting behaviour problems which affected both home and school life – none would have argued that their child did not cause difficulties at school. The parents also expressed considerable commitment to the pupils' education, and concern about the effects of them missing school. Several, like Mr Thomas, said they would like to help the pupil at home while they were excluded, but didn't know how to do it properly.

Given these factors there was a potential for partnership between parent and school in working to help the pupil and find strategies for coping with their behavioural difficulties. But the interviews revealed that where the pupil had been excluded, there had usually been little positive contact; though they often reported good relations with previous or subsequent schools.

Blamed, discounted, not listened to

Several points recurred when parents described contact with teachers. These often also applied, though to a lesser degree, to contact with other education professionals such as Educational Psychologists.

Parents talking to teachers about problems commonly received a list of complaints and felt *blamed* for the child's misbehaviour. For example the head teacher regularly tackled Ms. Collins about Roger's misdeeds at the school gate, in front of the other parents and children:

"I used to be terrified of going to that school because of the complaints, the constant complaints. It got me a nervous wreck."

Ms. Smith said:

"When I go up there they make me look really small, they make me feel small as if I'm the one that's in trouble ... they seem to talk down to me, they won't listen to me."

Indeed parents generally felt that they were *not listened to*: there was a one-way transmission of information. Ms. Smith put it this way:

"...People [should] listen to parents, they listen to what the parent has to say and not try and just push it under the rug because that is the attitude I got."

Others concurred:

"Every time we've gone down it's been like a quick statement and that's it, out, now I've got something to do, ...They talk to us but they don't ask us what we feel, about how we feel about what's going on." (Mr Thomas)

"...[I would] just listen to like what they said, oh Damian done this and the teacher was upset and we can't have this behaviour and things like that, you know." (Ms. Bishop)

Parents felt they were not usually *involved in decisions* about how the school handled the pupil's misbehaviour, especially the use of formal or informal exclusion. Yet the parents mostly felt that exclusions were not useful sanctions, concurring with Ms. Davis:

" I don't think it does the child any good at all, I think it's...they feel as though they've got away with it, you know."

Andrew Smith's mother was extremely angry that the residential school brought him home to her without warning or previous discussion at least twice for her to punish him. On one such occasion she arrived back from being out to find Andrew had been brought home and left by the teacher with a neighbour. In Anne's case, the school took the decision to exclude her permanently without reference to Social Services, the Barnardo's education project which was intensively involved, or the teacher who ran the on-site unit.

As an extension of this point, parents often had strong *views about their children's special needs and problems* which they felt were *discounted*. For example Roger's mother, like several others, thought her child might be hyperactive. She wanted him tested for food allergies, because she noticed his mood was affected by eating chocolate, and also for epilepsy which was in the family and caused mood swings and behavioural problems in a relative. But the child psychologist disagreed and so nothing was done. Several parents thought their child might be dyslexic but did not know how to pursue this.

Ms. Smith like several other parents was keen to discuss her child's emotional and behavioural problems and how they could be handled:

"...Andrew likes a one on one and he was getting that there [at the special education unit] for two hours and it takes him a lot of time to trust someone. I don't know why, I can't work it out, you know what I mean. And he had this teacher and then he was getting close to her and the woman changed her, see. I told them what he's like but they take no notice."

From the parents' perspective, then, schools seemed on the one hand to blame them for their children's misbehaviour at school, yet on the other to discount their ideas and concerns about the child's educational needs and problems.

Whose responsibility?

This was a difficult double bind for parents and probably reflected a difference between them and the schools about their relative roles and responsibilities in relation to their child's education and behavioural difficulties.

Parents commonly felt that however difficult their child, it was the job of the school – or failing that the education authority through an alternative placement – to find a way of controlling them and educating them during school hours. Use of exclusion as a punishment, or to implement a school's assessment that it could not contain a child, seemed like a way of dumping the problem on to them instead which they bitterly resented. Ms. Davis, whose son was regularly excluded from a special school, felt this strongly:

"Is there such a thing as a special school where they don't have to send the kids home?
...You get the impression as though a special school, they can deal with a violent child or a problem child but they don't, they seem to shift it off on to parents sort of thing.

...School and home should have been a separate thing ... in an area like this, school should be a firm solid base."

Ms. Smith complained:

"...I was getting phone calls every day, can you come and sort Andrew out. Now I thought schools were supposed to be there to be able to control children but from what I've seen of them, none of them can."

Dissatisfaction was exacerbated where pupils who were out of school for long periods received little or no tuition, and/or, as was common, parents had to take the initiative in demanding alternative placements. The school, and sometimes the education authority, often appeared to have passed responsibility for resolving the situation to the parents. As Ms. Bishop said:

"they [school] should be involved in it, they shouldn't just say oh he's not coming back."

Ms. Collins regularly asked the school and the education office for a special school place:

"...No disrespect to you, I says, but you can't contain him, I says. So he obviously needs a special school. He [head teacher] said well just keep going down to the education..
...I used to go down education and say well look, I've had to pick him up from school, what are you going to do about it?"

Michael, excluded in the afternoons for two terms, was only given work to bring home for the first few weeks. His father went to the school about it but

"They didn't want to know, they'd washed their hands of him."

Several parents contrasted the school which excluded with a previous or subsequent one which they saw as committed to resolving problems. The latter were all special schools or primary schools.

The family and exclusion

Family situation

Five of the six families were living on income support: the exception was Ms. Bishop who worked part-time. Four of the six were lone parents, at least in part reflecting the make-up of families using FSU and Barnardo's services. In addition to the inevitable financial stresses of bringing up children on the poverty line, ill-health and other family difficulties were common. In this context conflicts with the school were at the least an extra turn of the screw: at worst, the last straw.

Causes of emotional/behavioural difficulties

In all families, the parents linked the pupil's behaviour problems, in whole or in part, to previous family crises. These included bereavement (death of father or other relative – in two cases, much loved grandparents), separation from father, illness in the family and moving home. In most cases more than one of these had coincided. For example when Andrew was four his father left and his grandmother died within the year. Two years later the family moved and contact with the father ceased, and Ms. Smith felt this period was when Andrew's problems started. Michael had been deeply attached to a baby cousin and when he was nine was traumatised by seeing him die at home. Within a year his mother nearly died in labour, and his baby sister, hospitalised for some time after birth, required 24 hour attention because of a heart condition.

Effects of the exclusion: practical

Long-term exclusion resulted in financial problems. Parents complained of the difficulty of managing without free school meals, a significant additional benefit for families managing on income support. On their limited income they could not usually provide trips and extra amusements, which compounded the tensions in the home, although some did struggle to do so. In some cases heating bills went up.

Ms. Bishop had been working full-time before the exclusions. This caused problems when Donald was excluded in the dinner breaks as she had to rush home. Once Donald was excluded indefinitely she was told by Social Services (involved because of his difficult behaviour at home) that she had to drop to part-time in order to care for him. She was lucky that this proved possible in her case but as she said, jobs for lone parents are hard to find.

Effects of the exclusion: compounding other stresses

Having a difficult child at home full-time, and/or repeatedly excluded for short periods, was difficult for parents coping with other problems to bear. Ms. Davis, who had ongoing family problems as part of which some of her children spent periods in care, said that when Martin was excluded:

"You're dealing with the school problems plus the problems at home which combine, it's like having a bees' nest waiting to, you know, go off."

Ms. Thomas and her husband were asked to go to the school at at difficult time:

"She (headteacher) just said Michael's behaviour is terrible, we just don't know what to do with him any more. So then I just started crying because she(baby)'d just been rushed in hospital anyway and it was something I could have done without. I need Michael in school, I can never say when she's going to be in hospital."

Effects of the exclusion: tensions for pupils and parents

Anne, encouraged by her foster-mother, worked on her own in the public library while excluded. She was the only pupil to be positive about being excluded. The most common complaint from others was of boredom.

In most cases exclusion clearly heightened stress within the family. There were often family rows, caused by boredom on the pupil's side and tension on the parent's. As the Thomases put it,

"I get upset and then he gets upset, and he's got a habit of tormenting the little one." (Ms. Thomas)

"Boredom, you know what I mean." (Mr Thomas)

In two cases the parent became seriously depressed or the child became uncontrollable. It was generally felt by parents that they and the child both suffered. Ms. Davis explained:

"...dealing with the family problems and dealing with Martin and dealing with the education and God knows what else, I mean at the end of the day there were nobody there for me. I wasn't getting away from them, I weren't getting any time out and neither were Martin. He were suddenly going from going to school and being with boys and playing football and God knows what else they get up to, to being stuck at home with mum, brothers, sisters, nappies, bottles ..."

Where there were siblings, there could be jealousy of the pupil who was at home. In two cases, younger siblings began "acting up" as a result.

"...he thought oh, if I get into trouble I can stay at home. You see, that's the way all the younger ones see it, you know what I mean, like he's not at school, why have I got to go to school." (Ms. Smith)

Tensions were exacerbated where there was other illness in the family, as with the Thomases.

Conclusion

It will be seen that the interviews with Black and White families raise many common issues, especially around the labelling of pupils defined for various reasons as "difficult", and the alienation and disempowerment felt by parents. In addition the interviews with White families reported in this chapter raise other problems, which we do not see as confined to White families: our 30 case studies indicate that they are important across the range of families. Policy implications of these issues are discussed in chapter eight.

Exclusion as a coping strategy – for whom?

From our interviews it seemed that pupils were being excluded regularly and on a routine basis. The same pupils were often repeatedly excluded by the same or successive schools. Exclusion may well have seemed an effective immediate strategy in removing the problem in the classroom, but our interviews showed that the effect on the pupil, both educationally and personally, was always negative. The stress on the family was also often severe.

Special educational needs

The cases highlighted the problems caused by the exclusion of pupils with special educational needs. It appears that the educational system was unable to provide appropriately for these pupils, even though in some cases they were at special schools designed to cope with them.

Relations between schools, pupils and parents

As in chapter five, the White interviews reveal that parents and pupils felt a lack of power and rights in relation to education. The complex web of reasons for this needs to be disentangled. But an important factor is likely to be social class. Most of the families we interviewed lived in disadvantaged areas, and depended on state benefits: there are general issues of increasing social exclusion and marginalisation of such groups. As a result these parents and pupils are likely to have to struggle much harder to be heard than their middle class counterparts.

Pupils interviewed, like the Black pupils in chapter five, wanted their point of view to be listened to. Their complaints reflect the failure of education policy to emphasise the rights of children.

Exclusions and inequity

These interviews underline the points made elsewhere in the report about inequity. However problematic their behaviour, to exclude these pupils repeatedly or for long periods is to reduce their access to education thus in turn reducing their future life chances. The widespread exclusion of pupils with special educational needs (13% of permanent exclusions recorded by the DFE (DFE 1992) were of pupils with statements of need) could be seen as evidence to support those who argue that pupils with special needs are liable to be increasingly marginalised with the move towards schools competition and league tables. As Ms. Smith put it:

"I think that there should be more of these things in the schools for children with special needs. There should be more understanding towards them, not pushed to the back and saying "you're there"...because to me the whole system's completely wrong in these mainstream schools. They seem to have catered for the intelligent ones, sort of thing, never mind what happens to the other kids."

7. Summary of Key Findings

A number of key findings emerge from the case studies reported in this section. They supplement and reinforce the previous evidence of increasing school exclusion discussed earlier in the report, adding important insights drawn from families' experience and perspectives.

Types of exclusion

Our case studies show that some pupils are being excluded repeatedly, and in some schools formal or informal exclusion is being used as a routine sanction rather than a last resort.

Our findings support previous concerns about the widespread use of "informal" exclusion, including part-time exclusion, which bypasses official records.

The home and the school

The families we studied were often suffering from other stresses, including poverty, bad housing, illness or bereavement. In some instances such a home trauma triggered problems at school.

Exclusion was a considerable additional burden for families and could cause practical, financial and relationship pressures.

The parents, though concerned about their children's difficulties, often felt alienated from the school, looked down on by teachers, and powerless to influence how the school handled the situation. This seemed to be felt especially keenly by parents of Black children.

Parents of children with emotional and behavioural difficulties often felt blamed for their children's behaviour, though they themselves found it hard to contain. They felt the education system should be able to cater for their children's special needs.

Schools and pupils

The cases we studied included pupils out of school for long periods, with little or no educational input. Around half of the pupils had missed at least six months schooling, and two had been out of school for three years or more.

Pupils with statements of special educational needs were being excluded from mainstream and from special schools. Some extremely vulnerable young people were out of the educational system for long periods, with very negative consequences for them and for their families. In some cases studied the exclusion was a direct result of lack of special needs provision in the school.

Particularly when they were excluded for long periods, pupils suffered educationally and also in personal terms. Some got into serious trouble; others felt demoralised and lacking in self-esteem.

Pupils who felt unfairly blamed sometimes reported that they had little or no opportunity to put their side of the story.

Excluded pupils and their parents sometimes felt the exclusion occurred because they had been unfairly labelled as troublemakers by teachers. This came through particularly strongly in cases of Black pupils who also pointed out that when they retaliated to racist name-calling and other forms of racial harassment, this could provoke a series of events which led to exclusion.

We found evidence to suggest that similar behaviour by pupils could be treated in widely different ways by schools.

Most pupils in the cases studied liked school and wanted to be there. Those interviewed often expressed a liking for particular lessons and present or past teachers. Parents also described positive relations with certain schools.

Exclusion procedures

The cases we studied suggest that some schools do not follow the legal requirements for informing parents about exclusions.

Our cases also bear out other evidence of parents' general lack of information about their rights in relation to their child's exclusion.

They also point to parents' lack of power when negotiating with the school about exclusion or other problems.

The report also raises the question of the lack of appeal rights for the excluded pupil and the common difficulty for them in putting their side of the story, as well as their parents', when they felt unfairly accused.

PART THREE
POLICY DISCUSSION AND RECOMMENDATIONS[3]

---

[3] While this section draws on the whole report, and owes much to the work of all four authors, the policy discussion and recommendations remain the responsibility of Barnardo's and FSU.

8. Policy Discussion

This chapter draws out policy issues which arise directly from the find-ings outlined in chapter seven, and makes recommendations for change.

Policy implications of our findings

Types of exclusions

Our research provides examples of children's education which has been severely disrupted by exclusion, often used as a routine sanction rather than an action of the last resort. All exclusion acts to deny pupils their rights to education and to the full curriculum, and, as our case studies have shown, can also have disastrous effects in other areas of pupils' lives.

Our findings also support previous findings that:

"there is a population of pupils who find themselves on a spiral through the different categories of exclusion and who, subsequently, remain out of the system, on occasion untracked by the education authority" (OFSTED 1993a).

Our research also confirms previous findings that much exclusion is "informal" and unrecorded in official statistics. We found examples of repeated/long term exclusion at dinner breaks or for half days, regular informal exclusion for short periods without official notification, and parents being asked to withdraw their children to avoid permanent exclusion. Some pupils were also repeatedly excluded from lessons within the school.

Repeated formal or informal short-term exclusions have serious consequences for pupils, who are liable to find themselves unable to keep up with their class work as a result. This reduces their educational attainment and also is likely to demoralise and alienate them, thus storing up future problems in the classroom.

It is vital to find alternative sanctions and to look to preventing problems escalating to the point at which exclusion appears the only solution.

We recommend:

The DFE should establish a mechanism for the national monitoring of exclusions, and publish detailed figures regularly.

The DFE should commission research into the problem of exclusion, to examine both causation and the extent of associated phenomena such as informal, part-time and within-school exclusion.

The home and the school

Bad communication between teacher/school and parent often produces severe stress and frustration for both sides. Most importantly, the loser in the end is the pupil. Our case evidence highlighted the need to bridge the gulf between school and parents of pupils at risk of exclusion. The parents we studied often felt alienated and powerless; that they were not listened to, nor was their concern about their children's schooling recognised. Some parents of Black pupils expressed particular bitterness about how teachers treated them. Yet parents, like pupils, also reported good experiences with some teachers and/or schools.

Our cases also showed how *pressures at home,* such as poverty, poor housing, illness and relationship problems, affected both parents and pupils in their interaction with the school. We were also concerned that schools were sometimes unaware of or insensitive to significant traumatic effects within the family. We would argue that schools and teachers cannot ignore such pressures, and need to be working with others to reduce their effects on pupils' behaviour and achievement at school.

These issues require action on several fronts. On the one hand *teachers and schools need to be better equipped* to communicate with parents from all social groups. Time, support and training needs to be available for this, and the importance of teachers' pastoral role must be acknowledged. Schools should be encouraged to ensure systematic *early involvement* of parents whose children are presenting problems. Well-resourced education welfare services can play a crucial role.

We would also argue for *greater cooperation between education services and outside agencies* providing services for families and children. Teachers, schools and educational support services focus on pupils and parents in relation to the school while other professionals such as social workers have a primary focus on the home: yet both are working with the same families and often dealing with similar issues. There are many local examples of highly productive cooperation between schools and other agencies aimed at bridging the home/school gap – indeed both Barnardo's and FSU have local projects doing this kind of work. Inter-agency collaboration can provide innovative ways of linking parents and schools; while support/advocacy/counselling for parents from agencies independent of the education service can defuse or help to resolve actual or potential conflicts with the school. Both statutory and voluntary services can be involved in this.

In relation to statutory services, we would like to see closer collaboration between social services and education departments, as envisaged by the Children Act but often, in our experience, inadequately implemented.

We recommend a greater emphasis on pastoral care and inter-agency collaboration to overcome home/schools difficulties, together with dissemination of good practice in this area.

Parents of pupils with serious *emotional and behavioural difficulties* experience the problems described above more intensely than others. As indicated in chapters four and six, those we studied often felt blamed by the school for the difficult or unmanageable behaviour of their child, yet they themselves were often struggling to cope with this behaviour at home. Such pupils' bad behaviour was not straightforward naughtiness, nor could their parents simply control it by firm disciplinary measures. Just as these pupils, often vulnerable and distressed, need expert and adequate support rather than punishment, so do their parents. Adequate support in school for the pupil needs to be buttressed by adequate support for the parents – from statutory services such as education welfare, educational psychology and social services, as well as from voluntary services. Investment in these services is likely to provide good returns in terms of preventing the escalation of problems to crisis point.

Our awareness of the *interaction between home and school pressures* leads us to raise some broader questions about the overall emphasis and tone of education policy debates. Much of the recent public discussion about discipline in schools and parents' responsibility for pupils' behaviour tends to assume that parents whose children behave badly are wilfully neglecting their responsibility for controlling them. Exhortation backed up by punishment appears as the preferred method of changing this. By contrast we would wish to draw attention to the many-sided pressures on families in today's society, and to the links between such pressures – whether they be external, such as poverty or bad housing, or internal, such as relationship breakdown or abuse within the family – and how parents and pupils deal with schools.

Parents are currently under public scrutiny and the strength of family ties is being questioned. But both the cases we studied and our two agencies' general experience of working with families suggest to us that parents are usually committed to doing a good job and feel their responsibilities to their children strongly. We would like to see a greater emphasis on *support* for parents under pressure, to enable them to fulfil their responsibilities more effectively. And in line with the discussion above about links between schools and other agencies, we would also like to see greater links between education policy debates and other policy discussions in the field of social work and social welfare.

Schools and pupils

Avoiding the use of exclusion

Both parents and pupils in our case studies commonly reported positive relations with individual teachers and/or previous or subsequent schools, often in contrast with conflict with the school which excluded. This underlines the important point that in spite of external pressures on schools, not all respond by using exclusion to the same degree:

"There is an unacceptably wide variation between schools in the nature of the offence which leads to exclusion and in the rate of exclusion from individual schools, even taking account of their catchment area" (OFSTED 1993b).

This suggests that in spite of the difficult climate within which they operate, it is possible for schools to take steps to minimise the problem. Indeed, there are clear examples of schools where positive action has been taken, and in which an ethos which discourages exclusion has been developed.

Drawing on the recommendations of the Elton report there has been considerable discussion of the role of positive behaviour policies in helping schools to manage difficult behaviour without exclusion. Our study raises several issues in relation to the implementation of behaviour policies. Consistent application of these can be problematic because many rules require teacher interpretation, for example when pupils are excluded for disruption, defiance or insolence. In a number of the cases we studied this caused difficulty, as pupils felt they had been unjustly singled out. If schools have a positive behaviour code which identifies acceptable behaviour rather than long lists of rules which incur automatic sanctions, interpretative judgments cannot be avoided. But schools can work towards consistency by reducing the occasions on which individual teachers make interpretation, and reducing reliance on individual teacher judgments made in isolation. Good record keeping and thorough investigation, allowing the pupil accused of an offence to state their side of the story, is important and would have helped in some of the cases we studied.

We also recognise that in some of the exclusion cases we have reported, the school was criticised for treating pupils unfairly and not applying rules consistently, yet in others, especially where the pupil had emotional and behavioural difficulties, they were accused of operating rules too rigidly, ignoring the pupil's personal circumstances and problems. There seems indeed to be an inevitable tension between the need for decisions in relation to discipline to be consistent and fair, and the countervailing importance of flexibility and taking into account individual circumstances. This latter point is obviously particularly relevant where exclusion is at issue, and would suggest that any behaviour code needs to allow for flexibility in the application of sanctions. But it also underlines the complexities involved in constructing and implementing an effective behaviour policy, and the difficulty for the class teacher in balancing the needs of the individual pupil and the needs of the class as a whole.

We recommend that:

School behaviour policies should be designed to avoid the use of exclusion as a sanction wherever possible.

Research should be conducted to evaluate the effectiveness of school behaviour policies, and best practice should be disseminated.

Name-calling and racial harassment: forms of bullying

Our case evidence confirms that incidents precipitating exclusion often have a root cause which needs to be investigated to ensure fairness. Often the cause is name calling. Tizard et al (1988) found that 66% of eleven year old children attending inner-city schools say that they have been teased. Children need to know that they will be taken seriously if they complain. Allegations of name-calling need to be investigated and recorded. Failure to do so will be demeaning and undermining; the child's feelings of anger and despair will be bottled up creating the potential for a more serious disciplinary issue at a later date.

Investigation of name-calling is very important to all sort of children, including those with special educational needs.

In particular, racist name-calling was a serious issue for the Black pupils and parents we interviewed. Parents and pupils claim that schools ignore racial harassment, name-calling and bullying (as highlighted in our interviews, see also ACE 1992, Nottingham Education Department 1989). Where schools fail to investigate name-calling assiduously, they leave an opening for retaliation.

A commitment by the school that racist namecalling and related behaviour is unacceptable should be part of a commitment to equal opportunities. It has been shown that a clear stance by the school, to which all teachers are committed, can be effective in reducing racist name-calling (Troyna and Hatcher 1992). In this connection we welcome the DFE's specific reference in its draft circular on behaviour and discipline to the importance of tackling racial harassment and bullying (DFE 1993c). On the basis of our study we would ask schools to be particularly vigilant in ensuring that Black pupils accused of violence are not singled out for exclusion, where the violence is in fact a retaliation to racial harassment by other pupils.

We recommend that tackling name-calling and racial harassment should be an explicit priority in school behaviour policies

Equality of opportunity: other issues

We found that Black parents and pupils often felt strongly that the pupil had been unfairly treated. This underlines the need for equal opportunities policies to be integrated into behaviour codes, especially in the light of the evidence on teachers' interpretation of Black pupils' behaviour discussed in part one. On the basis of our evidence, we would also argue for the importance of stated equal opportunities policies alongside behaviour codes. Monitoring the impact of equal opportunities on the behaviour code requires the same attention to practical detail that has been previously described. This issue should not just be seen as affecting African-Caribbean pupils. In relation to exclusion, the national figures provided by the DFE do not give comprehensive information on ethnic origin and we have received anecdotal reports from staff that in certain areas exclusion of Bangladeshi pupils may be on the increase.

Although gender issues did not come to the fore in the cases we studied, there are clearly important questions to be asked in relation to gender and exclusion which we were unable to pursue in this study. Twenty-five of the 30 excluded pupils we studied were boys, compared with a national male/female ratio reported by the DFE of four or five to one (DFE 1992). In line with this, an even more extreme gender imbalance exists in special schools for pupils with emotional and behavioural difficulties (see for example DFE 1993d). We would like to see further investigation of this area.

Equal opportunities considerations extend beyond race and gender. According dignity and respect to every child involves recognising their cultural identity and their abilities. In the classroom this means that each teacher must address the ability range of the whole teaching group, otherwise children will be left to struggle. The school culture needs to place high value on according equal respect to all types of family, and to people from all social and ethnic groups; this will come through to parents as well as pupils.

We recommend that awareness of issues of race and culture should be promoted in initial teacher education, and in in-service training for teachers.

Classroom management

Our interviews and case studies pointed up pupils' feelings that some teachers 'labelled' them, or treated them in a contemptuous way. Once again, teachers need support in further developing the skills and understanding necessary for combining effective management of large groups with firm yet sensitive and respectful treatment of individuals, even where they are presenting difficulties of control. Relying on common-sense cannot be enough to handle the complexities involved. Looking at this area from a social work rather than an education perspective, we would regard classroom management in these situations as requiring high levels of skills and expertise.

The pupils in our study all reported that they got on well with some teachers. This indicates that some teachers are skilled in defusing confrontation. This is an extremely difficult area. Teachers are often dealing with volatile situations and sometimes with pupils presenting extreme behaviour. Behaviour which would be unproblematic in a smaller setting, with more possibility of individual attention, is likely to provoke chaos in a large class.

Special educational needs

Our cases raise worrying issues about the adequacy of support for pupils with emotional and behavioural difficulties, both in mainstream and in special schools. These include children with statements and the much larger population who may at some stage in their school career have special educational needs. In a number of cases the absence of sufficient support seemed to have led directly to these pupils being treated as 'naughty' rather than 'needy', and thus being excluded, even though their special needs had been clearly identified through the statementing process.

Our evidence would support the need for greater special needs resources, both within the school and for support services such as the education welfare and educational psychology services. Some of the cases we studied showed clearly that provision was being cut back. This raises questions about the effects of recent reforms of the funding and management of schools on the level and appropriateness of special needs provision.

We recommend that greater resources should be allocated for pupils with special needs. and that the exclusion of pupils with identified special educational needs is researched and monitored closely.

Exclusion procedures

The parents we studied often had little or no *information* about their rights in relation to exclusion, and usually felt powerless to challenge the decision. While recent and proposed changes to law and guidance may improve matters, they are unlikely to resolve the problem.

It is clear from our cases that parents needed support in challenging school decisions, and that most of those we studied did not feel appeal rights were of any practical use. We are pleased that the draft DFE guidance provides for schools to include, in the letter notifying parents of permanent exclusion, a list of *organisations available to advise and assist* them (DFE 1993e). We feel that it is important that in addition to advice from the education authority (for example from the education welfare service) independent advice should be available. But in our experience, in many areas there are few, or no, independent agencies at present with sufficient resources to advise and advocate properly. As discussed above, advice and advocacy for parents can be extremely positive for all parties, and its availability needs to be increased.

Our cases also highlight pupils' lack of rights. We note with regret that the 1993 Act does not provide legal rights for pupils of any age in relation to appeals against exclusion. We feel that the approach to children's rights embodied in the Children Act should be extended to education and that in principle the pupil should have the right to be heard in exclusion proceedings. This would be in line with Article 12 of the UN Convention on the Rights of the Child, emphasising the child's right to express views, which should be given "due weight in accordance with the age and maturity of the child," and encourages the principle that the child should be given the opportunity to be heard, whether directly or through a representative, in judicial or administrative proceedings which affect them.

We recommend:

The DFE should review current provision of advice and advocacy for parents and children, and ensure that such provision is available to all families facing exclusion.

Excluded pupils should be granted a right in law to be heard in an appeal relating exclusion.

9. General Policy Issues

Changes to exclusion law and guidance

The Education Act 1993 amended the law on exclusions, and just as this report was going to press, the Department for Education issued a draft circular on the subject, one of a number of draft circulars on "pupils with problems" (DFE 1993c-h). We are unable to respond here in full to the details contained in the circulars. However, we welcome the Government's recognition of the problem of exclusion and their desire to address it.

We have the following specific comments on the 1993 legislative changes, and on the proposals contained in the draft circular on exclusion (DFE 1993e):

We welcome the abolition of the use of indefinite exclusion and the limitations imposed on the use of fixed term exclusions.

Whilst the the removal of funding immediately a pupil is excluded will reduce the incentives for removing "difficult" pupils, we consider that the effectiveness of this should be monitored, and that, within a market framework, further disincentives to excluding may be required.

We welcome the greater regulation of out-of-school provision for excluded pupils but are concerned that such pupil referral units will not operate the full national curriculum. Not only is denial of access to the national curriculum likely to have negative implications for a pupil's educational achievement, it will make later rehabilitation into school more difficult.

We consider that the compilation of national statistics relating to exclusions is of vital importance in monitoring the problem and evaluating the effectiveness of policies designed to combat it. Given the Government's emphasis on the reporting of truancy, we are surprised that it should not regard the collection of data relating to exclusions to be of similar importance. We urge the Government to reconsider its position.

The proposed time limits on exclusion procedures and the detailed guidance on those procedures which are contained in the recent draft circular (DFE 1993e) are to be welcomed as providing fuller information for parents. The model procedures for schools to follow in instigating the exclusions should help to eradicate some of the worst practices. However, we consider that as far as practicable these requirements should be laid down in legislation. In many of the cases we studied, schools were apparently not following procedures set out in current guidance, and there is no reason to suppose that there will be greater compliance in following the new guidance.

Although these new measures should curb some of the bad practice in schools, they do not deal with the root causes of the escalation in exclusion. In addition to tighter legislative regulation and fuller guidance on exclusion, careful consideration, based on detailed research and analysis, needs to be given to establishing how best to support schools to cope with difficult pupils without resorting to exclusion.

Other policy issues

We consider that the increase in exclusions can only be understood in the context of changes discussed in chapter two: changes in education policy, limited resources for schools and teachers, and at the same time, wider social changes affecting families and children.

The present climate is not conducive towards supporting pupils whose behaviour is interpreted as challenging. Schools are increasingly subject to market pressures and judged by reference to league tables of academic achievements and truancy levels. Devolment of budgets to local management and the move towards grant-maintained status mean that schools have to choose between allocating resources to children with special needs and using them in ways which are more likely to gain them the status to attract and retain other pupils. Teachers may be demoralised as result of major change in education policies, cuts in resources and questioning of their professional competence. Public attitudes to children and young people have hardened and there is worrying emphasis on punishing rather than attempting to treat the causes of difficult behaviour.

Keeping all children in school implies allocation of more resources for pastoral care, for teachers to talk to parents, and for special educational needs. It requires sensitivity and skill on behalf on teachers, who themselves need to be adequately supported. It implies promotion of children's rights and incorporating the philosophy of the Children Act into education legislation. And most of all, it requires public and political recognition that exclusion not only has grave implications for those excluded, but for society as a whole.

sociological

10. Recommendations

For convenience, this chapter reproduces the recommendations which have been made at various points in chapter eight's policy discussion.

1 The DFE should establish a mechanism for the national monitoring of exclusions, and publish detailed figures regularly.

2 The DFE should commission research into the problem of exclusion, to examine both causation and the extent of associated phenomena such as informal, part-time and within-school exclusion.

3 There should be a greater emphasis on pastoral care and inter-agency collaboration to overcome home/schools difficulties, together with dissemination of good practice in this area.

4 School behaviour policies should be designed to avoid the use of exclusion as a sanction wherever possible.

5 Research should be conducted to evaluate the effectiveness of school behaviour policies, and best practice should be disseminated.

6 Tackling name-calling and racial harassment should be an explicit priority in school behaviour policies.

7 Awareness of issues of race and culture should be promoted in initial teacher education, and in in-service training for teachers.

8 Greater resources should be allocated for pupils with special needs, and that the exclusion of pupils with identified special educational needs is researched and monitored closely.

9   The DFE should review current provision of advice and advocacy for parents and children, and ensure that such provision is available to all families facing exclusion.

10   Excluded pupils should be granted a right in law to be heard in an appeal relating exclusion.

References

Advisory Centre for Education, 1993, *Findings from ACE investigation into exclusions*, London, ACE.

Audit Commission/HMI 1992, *Getting in on the act – provision for pupils with special needs: the national picture*, London, DES.

Barnardo's, *Response to Education White Paper "Choice and Diversity"*, 1992.

Bennathan, M., 1992, "The Care and Education of Troubled Children", *Young Minds Newsletter*, 10, March, 1992, pages 1-7.

Blyth E. and Milner J., 1993, "Exclusion From School: A First Step in Exclusion from Society?", in *Children and Society*, (1993) 7:3, pages 255-268.

Bowe and Ball with Gold 1992, *Reforming education and changing schools*, Routledge, page 137.

Commission for Racial Equality, 1985, *Birmingham LEA and Schools: Referral and Suspension of Pupils*, London, CRE.

Department for Education, 1992, *Exclusions: a Discussion Paper*, London, Department for Education.

Department for Education Press Release 1993a, "A New Deal for 'Out of School' Pupils", *Department for Education News 126/93*, 23rd April, 1993.

Department for Education 1993b, *Draft code of practice on the identification and assessment of special educational needs*, London, Department for Education/ Welsh Office, page 2.

Department for Education 1993c, *Pupil behaviour and discipline*, draft circular 1, "Pupils with problems", London, Department for Education/Department of Health, paragraph 51.

Department for Education 1993d, *The education of children with emotional and behavioural difficulties*, draft circular 2, "Pupils with problems", London, Department for Education/Department of Health, paragraph 14, paragraph 15, paragraph 120.

Department for Education 1993e, *Exclusions from school*, draft circular 3, "Pupils with problems", London, Department for Education/ Department of Health.

Department for Education 1993f, *The education by LEAs of children otherwise than at school*, draft circular 4, "Pupils with problems", London, Department for Education/Department of Health.

Department for Education 1993g, *The education of sick children*, draft circular 5, "Pupils with problems", London, Department for Education/Department of Health.

Department for Education 1993h, *The education of children being looked after by the local authority*, draft circular 6, "Pupils with problems", London, Department for Education/Department of Health.

Education for All: the report of the committee of enquiry into the education of children from ethnic minority groups, HMSO 1985.

Family Service Units, *Response to Education White Paper "Choice and Diversity"*, 1992.

Furlong, J.V., 1985, *The Deviant Pupil: Sociological Perspectives*, Milton Keynes, Open University.

Gains, C.W., 1993, "Editorial", *Support for Learning*, Vol. 8, No. 4.

Garner, P., 1993, "Exclusions: the Challenge to Schools", in *Support for Learning*, Vol. 8, No. 3, 1993.

Gillborn, D., *"Race", Ethnicity and Education – teaching and learning in multi-ethnic schools*, 1990, London, Unwin Hyman.

Graham, J., 1988, *School, Disruptive Behaviour and Delinquency: A Review of Research*, Home Office Research Study No. 96, London, HMSO.

Hansard 1993, col. 1667, 11.3.1992.

HMI 1991, *Standards of Education 1989/1990: the annual report of HM Senior Chief Inspector of Schools*, Department for Education.

Hutton, W., *The Guardian*, 27.1.1992.

John, P., 1993, unpublished M.A. thesis, University of the West of England.

Kumar, V., *Poverty and inequality in the UK: the effects on children*, National Childrens Bureau 1993, pages 15, 9, 141-3, 184-6.

Lloyd-Bennett, P., "Stockpiling the unsaleable goods", *Education*, 13.8.1993.

Lloyd-Smith, M., "Problem behaviour, exclusions and the policy vacuum", *Pastoral Care*, December 1993.

Longley, S. and Newsome, A., 1988, "Suspensions and Exclusions – Suggested Procedures", in *Pastoral Care*, December 1988.

MORI Survey reported in "A Class Apart", *Panorama*, BBC, 19th March, 1993.

National Union of Teachers, 1992, *The Response of the NUT to the Department for Education Discussion Paper on Exclusions*, London, NUT.

Nottingham Advisory and Inspection Service, 1989, *Pupil Exclusions from Nottingham Secondary Schools*, Nottinghamshire County Council, Nottingham.

OFSTED 1993a, *Education for disaffected pupils 1990-1992*, London, OFSTED, page 3.

OFSTED 1993b, *Achieving good behaviour in school*, London, HMSO, page 17.

Peagam, E., 1991, "Swings and Roundabouts: Aspects of Statementing and Provision for Children with Emotional and Behavioural Difficulties", in *Maladjusted and Therapeutic Education*, Vol. 9(3), Winter, 1991.

Rutter, M., Maughan, B., Mortimer, P. and Ouston, J., 1979, *Fifteen Thousand Hours*, London, Open Books.

Secondary Heads Association 1992, *Excluded from school: a survey of secondary school suspensions*, Bristol, SHA.

Special Children, Editorial, October 1993.

Stirling, M., 1993, "Second Classes for a Second Class", in *Special Children*, May 1993.

Stirling, M., 1992, "How Many Children are Being Excluded?", *British Journal of Special Education*, 19(4), pages 128-130.

TES 1992, "Warnock rethink on special needs", *Times Educational Supplement*, 10th July, page 5.

TES 1993, *Times Educational Supplement*, 28th May.

Unemployment Unit and Youthaid, *Working Brief*, 1993, issues 44 and 49.

Wood, P. and Hammersley, M., (eds.) 1993, *Gender and Ethnicity in Schools: Ethnographic Accounts*, Milton Keynes, Open University.

Wright, C., (1987) "The relations between teachers and Afro-Caribbean Pupils: Observing multiracial classrooms" in Weiner, G. and Arnot, M. (Eds.) *Gender Under Scrutiny: New Enquiries in Education.* London, O.U./Unwin Hyman Ltd.

Afterword
Sir Peter Newsam

Exclusion is an event, something that happens to school pupils. But exclusion also reflects an attitude of mind and it is that attitude of mind that is of crucial importance.

The report produced by Family Service Units and Barnardo's deals briefly with the attitudes that lie behind exclusion. The authors suggest that these attitudes may in part be a product of recent legislation with its emphasis on the market. That implies that we are dealing here with something that has been of significance recently.

The problem of attitudes and their consequences for pupils who do not conform to prevailing standards is of long-standing. As the decades go by, the attitudes behind exclusion may sharpen or soften and become more or less serious in their effects. But they are always there and have been over the 120 or so years of public education in this country.

The problem has seldom been so clearly expressed as by Edward Thring, Headmaster of Uppingham School, in a book published in 1885. The school was for boys only and he dealt in that book with the problem of exclusion that can occur within a school itself:

"It is an absolute necessity, a self-evident truth, that every boy, whatever his ability may be, should be intelligently cared for and feel himself so cared for. In so far as he is not, that boy is not at school."

If this seems obvious perhaps the most obvious thing about it is that, as anyone visiting schools can observe, there remain far too many children who are not at school in Thring's sense though they turn up regularly day after day after day.

In short, the relationship between school and pupil is inadequate.

Teachers are too busy or distracted to be more than 'clerks of works', in Thring's phase; forced to see their role as presiding over a curriculum rather than engaging with those that have to learn it. The educational consequences for the rejected pupil in these conditions may be quite as serious as conventional forms of exclusion.

On conventional exclusion, in dealing with academic performance rather than behaviour, Thring struck a note which is recognisable today.

"As soon as individual minds" he wrote "are not the province of a teacher's work, nor each separate difficulty his care, as soon as knowledge, rules, and memory engross attention, the rest follows. There is the prescribed packet to be learnt, if a boy does not learn it, it is no business of the clerk of the works, beyond punishing him for not doing it. This soon passes into a neglect of those who cannot, or will not, pigeon-hole the daily quota; this naturally advances to finding them very much in the way; the next step is that in the interest of the better boys (so runs the story) they must be got rid of. So the school failures are turned out, and great authority quoted to support the practice; and all the energy of the place is expended on the strong and active, who will distinguish themselves in the knowledge scramble."

In Thring's day, there were no league tables based on examination results, but it is not difficult to guess what he would have had to say about those.

So the problem of the attitudes that lie behind exclusion is not a new one. The Government has recently been busy producing circulars on the technical aspects of exclusion. These deal with who has the right to do what on what time-scale and with what rights of appeal. All this is useful but is of secondary importance. In tackling the problem of exclusion, the essential aim must be to remove the motives for excluding in the first place. At the same time, within schools attitudes need to be developed which reduce the need to exclude. That in turn means that, as Thring suggests, teachers, as a professional body, need to assume responsibility for all children, however difficult they may prove to be.

Once that wide professional responsibility is assumed, it rests with others to ensure that teachers have the means to carry out that responsibility.

This again, is not a new problem. In the mid-70's, to take one example, secondary school numbers in inner London were declining sharply. Schools had to compete for pupils to survive and a well-ordered school, then as always, was one of the first things a parent looked at when choosing a school. It was then that the heads of schools raised the question of who was to be responsible for the disruptive pupils that, "in the interest of the better" children, to adapt Thring's phrase, they wanted to be rid of.

The answer was to enquire of the heads what they needed to enable them to carry out their professional responsibility for all children. Confronted by this, the heads did not call for additional sanctions, a suggestion that seems to be trotted out from time to time. They did not do so because sanctions are only effective where there is already a sound basis of good behaviour and parental support. Where both these are lacking, to attempt to place a disruptive pupil in detention, for instance, is simply to invite defiance. The same applies to other disciplinary expedients. So the answer lies elsewhere.

London heads were clear about what they wanted. They wanted the means to place disruptive pupils in the care of teachers who were interested in their development, either within schools or at centres away from the main school premises. They asked to be made responsible for these centres, without undue intervention by the various psychological and other services that ordinarily become involved in such cases. Inevitably, these centres were labelled as "sin-bins", but this wholly misunderstood their purpose and functioning. The centres that then developed enabled some of the relationships, which Thring talked about, to be developed. Some times for the first time, disruptive pupils came to understand that there were adults interested in their progress and in themselves as individuals rather than the recipients of a curriculum. The response of the pupils was to attend regularly. Many soon came to be involved in the learning process itself. Often the skills were practical but always included elementary mathematics and literacy. One thing the centres achieved was to illustrate that all children, however unfavourable the prospect may seem, are able to learn if sufficiently motivated by skillful teachers. The chief drawback of the centres was that it was difficult to get the pupils within them to return to their ordinary schools. Their learning and motivation seemed to depend on the close concern, rather as in a family setting that many of them missed, with one or two individuals rather than with large numbers of other pupils and school staff.

How does that leave the problem of exclusion? In dealing with the attitudes that lie behind exclusion, obviously research evidence of the kind produced in this report is valuable. How is it that schools which rarely exclude achieve this? Is it because these schools exercise close control over their pupils through tightly enforced rules, school uniform and so on? Not in my experience. Low exclusion rates are associated with schools operating very different disciplinary procedures. The common factor in such schools is the one Thring pointed to all those years ago. Those working within the schools regard their relationships with all the pupils in their charge as their first priority; be they disruptive or simply slow to learn.

"A dull boy's mind", Thring once said "is a wise man's problem". So it is with pupils that disrupt the work of others. They are a problem, well enough; they also have problems and it is the teacher's function to do everything possible to solve them within the school setting. It is the function of those outside the school to help teachers carry out their responsibilities for all children; well or badly balanced alike.

Appendix
Overview summary of 30 case studies

1 Gender	M	F	Total
FSU	14	2	16
Barnardo's	11	3	14
Total	25	5	30

2 Race	Black	White	Total
FSU	7	9	16
Barnardo's	2	12	14
Total	9	21	30

Note that "Black" includes two mixed race and one Moroccan.
"White" includes one Irish Traveller.

3 Age/Schooling	Primary	Secondary	Total
FSU	9	7	16
Barnardo's	4	10	14
Total	13	17	30

Of the 13 primary age, all boys and 4 Black. Of the 17 secondary age,
12 boys of whom 3 Black, 5 girls of whom 2 Black.

4 Race by schooling by gender

Ethnic group	Primary		Secondary	
	M	F	M	F
Black	4	0	3	2
White	9	0	9	3
Total	13	0	12	5